COMPLIMENTS OF
The Bralove Group
Morgan Stanley
D0872163

BAGELS, SCHMEARS, AND A NICE PIECE OF FISH

BAGELS, SCHMEARS, AND A NICE PIECE OF FISH

A Whole Brunch of Recipes to Make at Home

CATHY BARROW

Photographs by Linda Xiao

CHRONICLE BOOKS

SAN FRANCISCO

Library of Congress Cataloging-in-Publication Data

Names: Barrow, Cathy, author. | Xiao, Linda, photographer.
Title: Bagels, schmears, and a nice piece of fish / Cathy Barrow ; photographs by Linda Xiao.
Identifiers: LCCN 2021035053 | ISBN 9781797210551
Subjects: LCSH: Bagels. | Cooking (Bagels) | Sandwiches.
Classification: LCC TX770.B35 B344 2022 | DDC 641.81/5--dc23
LC record available at https://lccn.loc.gov/2021035053

Manufactured in China.

Food Styling by Barrett Washburne.
Prop Styling by Maeve Sheridan.
Design by Lizzie Vaughan.
Typeset in Berthold Akzidenz Grotesk.

10 9 8 7 6 5 4 3 2 1

Chronicle books and gifts are available at special quantity discounts to corporations, professional associations, literacy programs, and other organizations. For details and discount information, please contact our premiums department at corporatesales@chroniclebooks.com or at 1-800-759-0190.

Chronicle Books LLC
680 Second Street
San Francisco, California 94107
www.chroniclebooks.com

TO MY MISHPOCHA

ORDER HERE

MY BAGEL LIFE

I grew up Jewish—gastronomically, culturally, and only marginally observant. My Boston-born mother, Jan, was not built for Toledo, Ohio, bemoaning a world without a seashore, an international airport, nor a single freshly baked bagel.

To remedy the situation, my grandmother Bea would fly to us regularly with provisions. As she exited the plane looking elegant in a trim suit, heels, and a chic hat, as if off the pages of a magazine, our eyes would be trained on the round, striped hatbox tied together with wide, white ribbon, stuffed to the brim with bagels from my mother's favorite Brookline bakery.

On the way home in the car, my mother, oblivious to the rest of us, would pry open the box, and the mountain of bagels would fill the car with a wonderful yeasty aroma. I gazed at the tiny poppy seeds, sesame seeds, flakes of onion, beads of garlic. Pumpernickel bagels, dark and sweet, contrasted with the sunny yellow egg bagels. Always, there were bialys, but only a couple. My mother worked to ferret out and take the first bite of the lone salt bagel. My mother loved bagels.

For my entire life, those have been the bagels by which I evaluate any others. Until very recently, finding a good bagel in much of the country was nearly impossible. The sad, spongy, pale, presliced offerings, usually frozen and steamed back to life, were downright unacceptable. A determined DIY-er, I struggled to make a bagel at home, one that could live up to my bagel standards. Time after time, recipe after recipe, they were doughy, they lacked the proper structure, and the flavor was dull. They were just rolls with holes. I began to wonder if maybe bagels were just one of those things that couldn't be made successfully in the home kitchen. But I persisted, fueled by the belief that there's nothing like freshly baked homemade bread—surely the same was true for bagels.

In 2016, the *Washington Post* printed a recipe for bagels that changed all that. I discovered the power of high-gluten flour, and from that recipe, I went on to find more than a dozen additional bagel recipes that led me to months of experimenting in the kitchen. Eventually, I had a bagel with the chew, the density, the tang, the consistency, and the yield that I wanted.

Once I conquered a solid basic bagel recipe, it was time to work bagel making into real life. After a few bakes, I gained competency, as one does with any skill, and my bagels consistently came out smooth and round with defined center holes. Soon, my experiments in the kitchen branched out into the deli offerings that accompany a great bagel. Naturally, the New York–style bagels began a kitchen journey that continued to seed-covered Montreal bagels, bialys, and oniony pletzels. I craved creamy schmears, sweet cured fish, and briny pickles, and before long, set out to produce the entire deli experience of my youth, right in my own kitchen. As I created different bagel flavor combinations, breakfast sandwiches and midnight bagel snacks became part of my bagel zeitgeist. *Bagels, Schmears, and a Nice Piece of Fish* distills the essence of these deli favorites into simple, easy-to-recreate recipes for a perfect bagel breakfast or an overstuffed bagel sandwich at any time of day.

MY MOTHER, JAN KADETSKY COHN

Whether you bake the bagels yourself or buy them and fill platters with homemade accompaniments, whether you dress up grocery store cream cheese or make it from scratch, I'll guide you through it all—including curing and smoking salmon, even if it's your very first time. Deli salads will evoke old memories or create new ones. And we will make half sours together, because when a bagel sandwich is lunch, a pickle spear belongs on the plate.

Throughout these pages you'll find that, in addition to the recipes, there are stories and asides, history and fables, and tales of my childhood. Because growing up, mine was a bagel-loving family in which every member could make a party from a bagel breakfast.

I did not start this project with the idea that writing and cooking my way through it would conjure memories of my grandparents, that I would again taste foods that we ate regularly when I was very young, or that I would suddenly start dreaming about those days. But that is precisely what happened. And because my world is larger now than it was when I was a child, I know that Jewish cuisine is defined not only in the Ashkenazi tradition, but also in Sephardic and other cuisines of which I have no direct experience. I leave that to other writers.

Mishpocha

My family encouraged a love of food and cooking, and found joy watching company delight in something homemade. I learned in kitchens that I can still see in my mind's eye—the big, white enamel stove with two ovens and a warming drawer, the Sunbeam mixer, the small paring knives with wooden handles I was allowed to use. I know you came for a cookbook, but you're going to get some family stories too. It's impossible for me to write about these foods and not see and hear my grandmothers in my ear. *Mishpocha* is Yiddish for family. It's a word filled with warmth. Meet the mishpocha.

My mother went to graduate school when I was three years old, teaching classes while she studied. My father was occupied with his work. So after school, during summer vacations, and on weekends, my brother, David, and I spent time with my paternal grandparents, Mary and Ben Solomon.

Until I was eleven years old, we lived near them. So near, in fact, that my brother and I could walk from our house—through a cornfield, across railroad tracks, winding through neighborhoods—and arrive at Grandma Mary's about twenty minutes later for a cold ice cream float or a cookie or hot cocoa. She spoiled us rotten in the very best way.

Born in Vilnius, Lithuania, Mary emigrated to Chicago with her seven siblings and grandmother just before the First World War. She learned to speak English without a trace of an accent, but peppered her sentences with Yiddish—the only one of my grandparents who did so. She never spoke of her life in Lithuania, which I fear might have been terrible. She came from a family of rabbis and leaders in the community, none of whom made the journey to America.

In the early 1920s, after completing eighth grade, Mary went to work for a stockbroker. She told me she "made a man's salary"—a point of pride her entire life. Her ambitions were cut short when her older sister Doris died shortly after giving birth to my father. Mary, in typical Old-World tradition, married her brother-in-law, my grandfather Ben, and left Chicago for Toledo, Ohio, to live as a housewife, volunteer, and savvy (but never acknowledged) finance manager for the family.

My Grandma Mary was a natural in the kitchen, comfortable with all kinds of cooking. She taught me to bake, to make chicken soup, and to remove the bones from a smoked whitefish. I still remember every corner of her kitchen, what was in each drawer, where she hid the licorice. Even well into my thirties, whenever I visited, she pushed a tin of brownies into my hand "for the trip home," an hour by airplane. What she called Aunt Sophie's Yum Yum Coffee Cake was so frequently on her kitchen counter that when I first saw a cinnamon swirl coffee cake in a bakery, I assumed somehow the store had my grandmother's recipe.

Every week growing up, we gathered at Mary and Ben's house with our family and their singleton friends for the Sabbath. Mary's Sabbath dinners were magnificent feasts of meats and vegetable-rich side dishes, homemade noodles or potatoes, and pickle plates. She spent Fridays setting the table with china and crystal and polishing the silver candlesticks. She served a first course of herring or smoked fish sitting atop cucumber slices or chopped liver spread across thin slices of challah. And after the meal, we watched *The Wild Wild West* and *Star Trek* with Grandpa Ben, an avid fan of both.

MY PATERNAL GRANDPARENTS, BEN AND MARY SOLOMON

I began research for this book by opening an army-green, dented metal box and thumbing through Mary's yellowed recipe cards. Her cramped writing, so familiar, listed ingredients and steps for favorite salads and luncheon casseroles, cakes and cookies, long-simmered stews, and thick soups. Apple cakes for Rosh Hashanah and matzo meal cakes for Passover. The origins of the recipe were noted in the upper-right corners, and here I found reminders of her Aunt Sophie, her sisters Mae and Rose, and her best friend, Faye Edelstein. The cards detailed adjustments she made to favorites, such as swapping in skim milk for cream and egg whites for whole eggs in a futile attempt to keep Ben's weight down.

My Grandpa Ben was a gourmand. Born in Chicago and raised in California, he liked to tell me about a childhood spent selling gleaned fruit on the Los Angeles streets. He did anything to survive. At the age of eighteen, he moved to the Michigan-Ohio border, where he started a business selling off the parts of a truck that he continued to sleep in until he could afford to buy another.

By the 1960s, he was traveling the world selling truck parts. While jetting around, Ben never met a cuisine he wouldn't try. He had an argumentative digestive system but blithely ignored the pain and indulged whenever he could. He returned from Europe with cheeses and wine, cured meats, and fancy chocolate. His trips to the Middle East yielded spice blends, pistachios (a rare treat), dried fruits, halvah, and Turkish delight. From Japan, he brought sakes, teas, rice crackers, and sesame snacks. He was generous and burly and made friends easily.

My strongest memories of Ben have him at the head of the Sabbath dinner table, wielding a carving knife and declaring the roast or leg of lamb or brisket a "nice piece of meat," the nugget that begat the title of this book. He lost his eyesight as he aged and depended on others to get him places, but his wanderlust and curiosity never dampened.

On my mother's side, my grandparents Bea and Allan Kadetsky were first-generation Jews descended from Russians. They were, in the middle of the American Century, working very hard to assimilate. They did not attend Temple. They ate shellfish and pork. They had a Christmas tree. Yet they hung on to certain gustatory traditions. Elegant Grandma Bea knew how to set out a proper bagel-and-lox brunch. Her chopped liver and chicken soup were magnificent. I didn't learn the family secret until I was in my thirties; she flavored her matzo balls with bacon fat. Shanda!

In my mind, my Grandpa Allan will forever be Mr. Martini: He smelled like Old Spice, tobacco, and gin. He taught me to crack a lobster, to dig in the sand for clams, and (at age six) to slurp oysters and beer at Boston's Old Oyster House. After retirement, he learned Szechuan cooking by watching PBS television shows. There's something distinctly Northern European about his Onions and Eggs (page 177), and I suspect it is something his Russian-born mother, Rebecca Wallockstein Kadetsky, may have made.

ALLAN AND BEATRICE KADETSKY

No one on the Kadetsky side was an all-around great cook. They had grown up in different times and circumstances, and for a few years around 1936, they even had a cook who lived in (a common occurrence in the previous generation, and one they held on to as long as they could). This is the way of the Kadetskys. Allan and Bea were post-1929-crash broke, as was the rest of the family, so they decided to pool their modest resources and, sensing a good deal, rented a sixteen-room mansion in Brookline, Massachusetts. Their neighbors on one side were the heirs to the Singer sewing fortune; on the other side lived Harry "Doc" Sagansky, a notorious gangster, who received late-night deliveries of what appeared to be bags of money.

Everyone lived there: My mother told me stories of the joys of growing up in this crazy house where she and her brother were entertained by their parents, grandparents, uncles, and aunts. Add in the cook and chauffeur (although there was no car; the two were married and came

In background, left to right:
MY GREAT-GRANDMOTHER AGATHA SOLOMON, BROTHER DAVID SOLOMON, GRANDMOTHER BEA KADETSKY, ME, MY MOTHER JAN COHN, AND MY GRANDMOTHER MARY SOLOMON

as a pair), and it's a scene from a madcap Frank Capra movie. For a while, there was even a Great Dane; that did not go well. In time, Bea and Allan left the enormous house, moved to a modest apartment, opened a children's clothing store, and lived like normal people.

As a family, my mother, father, David, and I visited the Boston relatives two or three times a year. Each visit was a wild ride of exotic foods for me. Whether we were digging clams at the seashore or wandering the Italian markets tasting gelato and cannoli, ordering ice cream sundaes at Schrafft's, picking wild blueberries in Maine, or wrestling massive lobsters into pots, I was encouraged to taste and learn, to ask questions.

It's only now, after spending time with these memories, that I've come to understand how my grandparents fed me far beyond the table. My gratitude is boundless; they are long gone, but their influence lives on in my heart and here, in these pages.

A HOMEMADE BAGEL BAKERY

Replicating a New York City Bagel

In the 1980s, a good bagel was hard to find in my hometown of Washington, DC. I traveled often to New York City for business, and I'd stay overnight to hang out with a gaggle of friends. Our late nights ended at the aptly named Tumble Inn. The following morning, in a 6 a.m. brain fog, I relied on coffee and a freshly baked everything bagel schmeared with chive cheese and stacked with satiny lox for my train ride home. This is my bagel order, and while I no longer stumble out of the Tumble Inn, a bagel lox sandwich never fails to remind me of those train rides.

In recent years, all across the United States, many cities and towns have welcomed new bakers and the bagels have improved. New offerings aside, I was determined to make bagels at home. With the help of that 2016 *Washington Post* recipe and subsequent deep dives down bagel rabbit holes on YouTube, reddit, and Google, I produced better bagels as I continued to tinker. I adjusted the temperature of the water, varied the rising times, and tried overnight bulk fermentation. I made small changes in the amount of water and yeast. I added salt and subtracted salt. I tested different sweeteners, diastatic malt powders, vital wheat gluten. I grew attached to and then utterly dependent on my kitchen scale, and that is why throughout the bagel recipes in this book, you will find gram measurements leading. Even water is given in grams. I think in grams now.

Trial and Error

After more than a year of this experimentation, I found my perfect bagel. It was small and fit in my hand like the bagel of my memories. But one bagel did not satisfy and two bagels were too many. Which begs the question: What is the right size for a bagel?

When I lived in Pittsburgh in the 1970s, a pack of us would walk from high school to Bagel Land in Squirrel Hill almost every day. There were bins as big as shopping carts, full of bagels. I loved watching the bakers in that bagel shop of my youth. They made two at a time, rolling chubby cylinders of dough under their two palms, flipping their hands with panache, and twisting the rope into a circle.

REAL TIME TALK ABOUT THE SLOW RISE

The Dilemma

Bagels need a slow, cold rise to develop flavor, yet the proteins in the flour give them oomph. They are so anxious to rise at room temperature that they can overproof in the blink of an eye. This means making bagels requires some planning.

HERE'S HOW I TIME IT OUT

8 PM
Mix and shape the dough.

7 AM
Start the oven and boiling water.

8 AM
Bagels, fresh, hot, and ready!

8 AM
Mix and shape the dough.

7 PM
Start the oven and boiling water.

9 PM
Bagels will be baked and cooled.
Place in a paper bag until morning.

They slid each dough circle over all four fingers, one on each hand, seam underneath, and rolled the bagels against the worktable, sealing the circle and tightening the crust. It's a dance under the palms.

We would order whatever had just come out of the deck ovens or wait until the next batch emerged. Those bagels were so hot we could hardly hold them. They cost 12 cents and probably weighed, before baking, about 80 g. Once baked, they were about the size of a tennis ball. Over the course of fifty years, bagels I encountered grew larger and larger, many wider than my palm and weighing in at well over 150 g. A couple of years ago, I ordered a bagel in an airport and was handed something so enormous, I could have sliced it like a pizza and fed a small household. I knew I had to find a middle ground. The bagels on the following pages weigh between 95 g and 130 g, the heavier ones made so by add-ins like raisins or granola. I love this size for breakfast or sandwiches. When I'm hosting brunch, I'll add half-size mini bagels because they're fun and it's possible to eat two without guilt.

While developing the recipes in this book, I confronted questions of not only size, but also yield. Our small household didn't need nine or ten or twelve bagels at a time. (I could freeze them, but let me show you my freezer sometime and then we can revisit that idea.) I struggled to fit multiple baking sheets in the refrigerator for an overnight rise. Who has that kind of space? In time, I scaled the recipes to yield a half dozen. Six bagels fit on a quarter-size baking sheet to proof.

Nowadays, somewhere in the midst of making dinner, I pull out the mixer, the scale, and a baking sheet. I measure flour, water, yeast, salt, and sweetener into the bowl. The mixer's dough hook kneads while I tend to other things. Forming the bagels takes only a minute or two and I tuck them into the refrigerator until morning.

Baking bagels as the coffee brews means the kitchen smells sensational. If you harbor fond memories of bagel bakeries, this will delight every one of your senses. I wake up on bagel mornings and leap out of bed because I can't wait to dive into that warm, yeasty, slightly sweet scent.

Not too many years ago, bakeries offered only plain, salt, poppy, sesame, onion, and garlic topped bagels. Latecomers pumpernickel, cinnamon raisin, and egg soon were everywhere. An everything bagel, which seems ubiquitous today, is a fairly recent—and entirely welcome—addition to the "OG Bagel" family.

Now, in the modern world of bagels, there are many flavor options, some of which would be all but unthinkable to my mishpocha, but if that's your thing, don't let me harsh your yum. I have trouble even imagining my grandmother's face if offered an Asiago Cheese and Pepperoni Bagel (page 87). Sure, Bagel Land would serve green bagels on St. Patrick's Day, but I don't remember Hatch Chile Jack (page 91) or Granola (page 74) bagels. Those are what I call Bagels My Grandmothers Wouldn't Recognize (page 71). For this book, I needed to broaden the field. I've dipped into the world of flavored bagels and, in truth, I've come to love them, especially for sandwiches (see pages 185 to 192) and piled high with a deli salad (see pages 152 to 165).

For those of you with gluten- or wheat-intolerance issues, I made sure to include a Gluten-Free Bagel (page 71). The qualities we love in a bagel, like a crisp outer shell and a good chew, are dependent on high gluten and they are challenging to replicate without it. This recipe makes a gluten-free bagel that's pretty darn close to a classic New York bagel.

Any bagel book has to include a couple of outliers, without which no bagel brunch would be complete: The Bialy (page 67), a chewy, floury, oniony roll, and The Pletzel (page 63), a soft and squishy bread to add to the basket of offerings at your next bagel brunch. A pletzel is airy and tender like a focaccia, with an onion topping, and goes hand in hand with herring.

A bagel-centric breadbasket is the beginning of a wonderful breakfast. When it arrives at the table right from your own oven, it's even better.

TACHLIS

THE PRACTICAL DETAILS

Bagels are deceptively easy to make. Break them down to the brass tacks, tachlis in Yiddish, and they require only five ingredients, none of which is exotic.

1. *High-Gluten Flour*

its high protein content contributes to a tight crust

2. *Malt Sweetener*

adds aroma and color, as well as flavor

3. *Yeast*

activates the rise

4. *Salt*

elevates the flavor, particularly a small crystal that dissolves easily

5. *Water*

hydrates the dough, contributing to the bagel's structure

For years, I tried to understand the science behind the perfect bagel. I wondered whether it was the New York City water, as I had always read, that made their bagels better. I even brought home a bottle of NYC's water to experiment, only to bake what amounted to a dinner roll with a hole, no signature snappy outer crust.

It's all about the high-gluten flour!

ESSENTIAL INGREDIENTS

Flour

The type of flour makes all the difference in bagel making. High-gluten flour brings the chew, the glossy exterior shell, and the dynamic rise that responds to a water bath and high-temperature baking.

"High gluten" on the label refers to the protein content—a whopping 14.2 percent. (Generic all-purpose flour has only a 10.3 percent protein level.) Those proteins create extra gluten strands, which make bagels delightfully chewy.

High-gluten flour is widely available, particularly online and through restaurant supply stores, if you can find a way to store 50 lb [23 kg]. I used Sir Lancelot Hi-Gluten Flour from King Arthur Baking Company to develop the recipes in this book.

If keeping assorted flours in your pantry is impractical, stash away a jar of vital wheat gluten for boosting the protein of all-purpose flour instead.

Pumpernickel, rye, whole-wheat, oat, and other specialty flours are far easier to source these days with broad access online. But the aroma, the color, and the unique flavor from flours that have recently been milled yield undeniably better results. If you live in an area with a flour mill, make it a point to visit.

Make Your Own High-Gluten Flour

All-purpose flour + vital wheat gluten creates a high-protein flour that turns out delicious bagels. Vital wheat gluten is the protein found in wheat and is available in powder form at a very reasonable cost. Also, it has a very long shelf life.

High-gluten flour can be made at home by whisking 5.5 g [2 tsp] of vital wheat gluten into every 120 g [1 cup] of all-purpose flour. For example, the New York Bagel recipe (page 43) calls for 420 g [3½ cups] of high-gluten flour. Instead, substitute with 420 g [3½ cups] of all-purpose flour into which you've whisked 19 g [7 tsp] of vital wheat gluten.

Sweeteners

Whether New York or Montreal style, all bagels require a sweetener. Malted barley (syrup or powder) is the most widely used, delivering the familiar bagel-ish taste and aroma. Some bagel bakers use sweeteners in both the dough and the water. My recipes call for the sweetener in the dough only (with the exception of Montreal style). If the bagel isn't sweet enough for your taste, next time stir 126 g [⅓ cup] of sweetener into the boiling water bath.

Barley malt syrup may be the most vexing, sticky, difficult ingredient in the kitchen, yet it is the most widely recommended for an authentic bagel. To accommodate its recalcitrant nature, take the syrup from the refrigerator and let it warm up ahead of any bagel baking. Pour it directly into the mixing bowl (set on the scale) aiming for the weight needed. Use scissors to portion the correct amount. If using a tablespoon measure, make sure the measuring spoon is sturdy and won't bend or break, and oil the spoon lightly before pouring the syrup from the jar. Barley malt syrup should be refrigerated once opened and is impossible to portion out when cold.

Some people "just can't" with the barley malt syrup; it's absolutely too sticky. I'm not going to insist, because there are alternatives:

Non-diastatic malt powder, a by-product of barley processing, will lend the right flavor and color. Subbing it into a recipe is easy: 1 Tbsp of malt powder substitutes for 1 Tbsp of barley malt syrup in the dough. And consider adding 1 Tbsp to the boiling water bath for extra oomph and to make the house smell like a true bagel bakery. *(Diastatic malt powder is a different ingredient and should not be used in bagel making.)*

Honey can stand in as a sweetener in any bagel recipe and is always used for Montreal style. The flavor of the bagel will not be malty but will reflect the floral or woodsy scent of the honey.

Cane syrup is a good substitute, as is Lyle's Golden Syrup, and both will flavor the bagel with light caramel notes.

Maple syrup is a delicious intentional substitute in The Cinnamon Raisin Bagel (page 57) and can stand in for the barley malt syrup in any recipe. It will change the flavor of the bagels, making them sweeter without the undertone that barley malt provides.

Although they resemble the look of barley malt syrup, molasses and sorghum are too rough and tumble to use as a substitute and I do not recommend either one.

Yeast

A few years back, I began using SAF-Instant Yeast. It is what all the cool kids (and the pros) use, and I jumped on the bandwagon. Boy, am I glad I did! It's dependable, consistent, and affordable. Instant yeast does not need to be bloomed in water and is, instead, added directly to the dry ingredients. It comes in a 1 lb [500 g] red package, recommended for breads. There is also one that comes in a gold bag, recommended for sweet dough recipes like sticky buns.

What seems like a considerable amount of yeast will stay viable for a year. I keep it in a tightly capped jar in the freezer and scoop out what I need.

Grocery stores sell two common types of yeast: active dry and fast-rising, typically available in foil three-packs or a squat dark glass jar. You can use active dry yeast interchangeably with instant yeast in my recipes, but plan to bloom the active dry yeast in 112 g [½ cup] of warm water before using, and reduce the water in the recipe by 112 g [½ cup]. When the yeast foams, after about 5 to 10 minutes, proceed with the recipe. If it does not foam, the yeast may no longer be effective and should be discarded.

Fast-rising yeast does not work for bagels; the dough proofs too quickly, leaving your beloved bagels tasteless and dull without the characteristic exterior crust.

Fresh yeast sold in foil-wrapped cubes is available in some places. I have never been able to find it easily and I have not worked with it, so I do not recommend it for any recipes in this book.

Sourdough

Sourdough leavening is another option altogether. Many modern bakers are using levains and starters to create signature bagels. I will admit to being a bagel purist: I'm not a fan of the sour flavor in my bagel. But don't let my predilection discourage your own experimentation!

If you are a veteran sourdough baker, you probably know that a good rule of thumb for replacing yeast with sourdough starter is to adjust the flour and water quantities in the recipe to account for the amount of each that is present in the starter.

In any of the bagel recipes, replace the yeast with 150 g [5¼ oz] of fresh, lively sourdough starter. Assuming the starter is made with equal parts water and flour, reduce the flour (high-gluten or all-purpose) by 75 g [2¾ oz] and the water by 75 g [2¾ oz].

Mix and form the bagels as instructed in the recipe. Rather than immediately refrigerating the formed bagels, leave them out, covered, to ferment on the counter for 2 hours. After that, refrigerate them for an 8- to 12-hour slow rise. Bake as usual.

PUMPER-
NICKEL
FLOUR
NET WT 48 OZ (3 LBS) 1.36kg
100241F01D 208813
EMPLOYEE-OWNED
We are 100% employee-owned and operated by a group of over 300 passionate bakers.
Certified B Corporation
We're a Certified B Corp — one of 3,200 companies that are committed to using the power of business as a force for social and environmental good. We leverage profit to create a positive impact for people, community, and the environment.
BAKER'S HOTLINE
WE'RE HERE TO HELP
Call or chat online with our friendly, experienced bakers.
855-371-BAKE (2253)
KingArthurBaking.com/bakers-hotline
* Why gluten-forming protein matters in flour: The amount of gluten-forming protein in flour determines the final structure of your baked goods. Higher protein flour creates more gluten, for a chewier structure, while lower protein
Kosher
The versatile,
gourmet salt
of choice for
Kosher cooking-
holiday time or

This method will need tweaking in your own kitchen, with your own sourdough starter and ambient temperatures. Play around. You may need to increase the amount of starter to 200 g [7 oz]. Or add in ¼ tsp of instant yeast for a little boost. If you are determined to use a sourdough starter, you will figure out the right balance for your unique environment.

Salt

Salt is surprisingly variable in both weight and flavor. The sheer saltiness can vary. I use Diamond Crystal kosher salt in my kitchen. It's neither fine nor coarse, but something right in the middle. It dissolves readily. I know how to use it instinctively. I know what my personal pinch of salt from the salt cellar will do for a pan of vegetables and I know how much to sprinkle over a freshly sliced summer tomato.

You likely have a favorite salt too. Perhaps you use Morton's kosher salt. To my taste, it is far saltier! Which makes sense because it weighs almost twice as much as Diamond Crystal. This means that your pinch of salt will deliver twice the salty taste.

When it comes to baking, too much salt can ruin a brownie or an angel food cake, and it can make a bagel, with so few ingredients, entirely unpalatable.

When it comes to pickling, the difference between these two kosher salts can be staggering. Sour pickles (page 169) made with my recipe and Morton's kosher salt will be inedibly salty.

Curing lox (see page 143) is another salty pursuit with the same speed bumps. For this reason, if you are a Morton's kosher salt household, please reduce the salt in every recipe by half. Add more salt only after tasting.

Kosher Salt Weight by Volume

KOSHER SALT BRAND	DIAMOND CRYSTAL	MORTON'S
¼ teaspoon	0.7 grams	1.2 grams
1 teaspoon	2.8 grams	4.8 grams
¼ cup	36 grams	60 grams

Fine sea salt weighs about the same as Diamond Crystal and is a ready substitute in every recipe.

Iodized salt has the potential to leave a metallic taste in baked goods and is chemically unsuited to pickling and curing. It should not be used in any of the recipes in this book.

Water

Bagel lore has perpetuated the myth that bagels cannot be made without New York City water. I am here to disabuse that myth. However, water remains one of the five essential elements of bagel making, so if your water has a heavily metallic or sulfurous taste, opt for filtered water instead.

In the following recipes for bagels and other breads, I've listed water in both volume and weight (grams). I recommend weighing all ingredients, and especially the ingredients in bread baking.

TOOLS OF THE TRADE

Stand Mixer

When I first set out to make bagels, a bagel baker asked me, "Are you making bagels in a home mixer?" When I answered yes, he shook his head and said, "Not for long."

Yet, for several years, I have managed to make bagels at least once a week with my trusty KitchenAid mixer with no ill effects. Admittedly, I have the bowl-lift, 6 qt [5.7 L] "professional" model with a big motor. The other type, with the tilting head, has a less powerful motor and while it will knead the sturdy bagel dough, it is prone to walking across the counter, so stay close. For the weekly or occasional bagel baker, any stand mixer will work perfectly well. Making dozens of bagels at a time will take a toll on any mixer; eventually the pull of the heavy dough will wear out the gears.

Bagel dough requires a long knead—I recommend at least 7 minutes. Some recipes recommend 15 minutes. That's a lot of work for your mixer's little motor. If you have dreams of making and selling boxes of bagels from your kitchen, you may need to invest in a more substantial machine.

If it seems as though the mixer is making a huge effort, transfer the dough to an unfloured work surface and knead it by hand until smooth, satiny, and bouncy, 15 to 20 minutes. Bonus: This will count as your daily workout.

Kitchen Scale

A digital kitchen scale is the most useful tool in my kitchen. It guarantees that success with a recipe can be repeated. It means precision and accuracy.

A kitchen scale also means fewer dishes. Seriously. With a kitchen scale, when the bagels go into the refrigerator, there is only a teaspoon, bowl, dough hook, and flexible bench scraper that need to be washed. If consistent outcomes aren't enough to convince you to get a scale, surely reducing the number of bowls and spoons to wash might do it?

To use, place the bowl from the stand mixer on the scale and tap the TARE key to return the display to zero. Weigh the flour, tare again. Weigh the water, tare again. Weigh the sweetener, tare again. Spoon in the yeast and salt.

When grocery shopping, purchase ingredients by weight and there will be less food waste.

Baking Sheets

After the kitchen scale, my quarter-size baking sheets may be the most used items in my arsenal. Most of us have baking sheets that measure 13 by 18 in [33 by 46 cm]. In the restaurant kitchen, those are called half sheets. A quarter sheet is 9 by 13 in [23 by 33 cm], and just 1 in [2.5 cm] deep. I have a stack of them and use them for everything from organizing ingredients for a mise-en-place to baking slab pies to serving friends their own personal cocktail hour drinks and snacks.

Some baking sheets are packaged with a rack that fits inside, which is useful for drying a piece of salmon before smoking. Some baking sheets come with snap-on covers—I use those for overnight proofing. Six bagels fit for proofing on a quarter sheet pan.

Quarter sheet pans aren't essential, but the size is more accommodating to smaller refrigerators.

Baking Steel or Pizza Stone

In a bagel bakery, deck ovens create the ideal environment to encourage the customary shiny shell that surrounds a really good bagel. Like a pizzeria oven, these ovens can be tile- or brick-lined and are often wood-fired. Their low profile keeps the heat radiating close to the bagels.

I experimented with convection, steam, and other adjustments to trick out my oven. When I turned to the Baking Steel, a tool I have written about for years, I was able to emulate the deck oven's radiating heat. The bagels baked on the very hot Baking Steel surface had a shell all the way around without being turned over mid-bake. The crumb was ideal. My search was over. If you have a pizza stone, it works in the same way.

More Kitchen Gadgets

All these items are nice-to-haves, not need-to-haves. They're widely available from a variety of sources, either online or in stores.

Parchment paper: The most economical option for parchment is to buy precut 13 by 18 in [33 by 46 cm] sheets, usually sold in packs of one hundred or boxes of five hundred. They are available at restaurant supply stores and online.

Skimmer or spider: A wide, perforated skimmer, often called a spider, is the right tool for lifting bagels from the water bath. You'll find many other uses for it too.

Instant-read or digital thermometer: A kitchen thermometer is endlessly useful, whether checking the steak on the grill or bread in the oven.

Bench scrapers, both flexible and stiff: An extension of the baker's hands, a flexible bench scraper will clean out a bowl, lift and transfer dough, and even move chopped vegetables from the cutting board to the skillet. A stiff bench scraper cleans the floury work surface, divides and portions stiff doughs, and chops sticks of butter.

Plastic bread bags or baker's bags: These can be purchased in packs of one hundred with twist ties. They are much more affordable than zip-top plastic bags.

Fabric bread bags: These are a green alternative to plastic bread bags; cotton and linen are best.

Beeswax wraps: These are another green alternative to plastic bread bags.

Classic bread boxes: Made out of wood, steel, or ceramic, these old-fashioned items reliably control the humidity to keep bread fresher, longer.

Tea towels or cheesecloth: I save my oldest, most threadbare, all-cotton or linen tea towels to use and reuse in cheesemaking. Cheesecloth is often available in the grocery store if you're fresh out of old threadbare towels.

Wood chips: For smoking. You can find these online, or source them from your own fruit trees, if you are lucky. Only use well-seasoned, aged wood in the smoker. Indoor smokers use smaller wood shavings specially designed to work on the stovetop.

№1

CLASSICS 43

BAGELS

BAGELS MY GRANDMOTHERS WOULDN'T RECOGNIZE 71

HOW MANY SIDES HAS A BAGEL? AN INSIDE AND AN OUTSIDE. —JEWISH RIDDLE

SINCE THE LATE 1600s, the bagel has been both a celebratory bread and a daily bread, managing to bridge all parts of society. There is evidence of early round celebratory breads baked in Turkey (see The Turkish Simit, page 53), but they are not boiled before baking, and therefore cannot be classified as a true bagel. Researcher Maria Balinska, writing in *The Bagel*, cites a Yiddish source dated 1683 as the first written mention of bagel (baigel, baygel, beygel) baking in a Polish town in what was then a slippery border between Russia and Germany. There had been a Turkish invasion in the years before this mention, thus the debate. Most likely, it was in this Polish town where round breads, uniquely boiled before baking, became part of the culture.

In the United States, bagel bakeries opened wherever Jewish immigrants landed—Brooklyn, Boston, Philadelphia, Baltimore, Charleston, Atlanta, Pittsburgh, Detroit, Chicago, and farther west.

Before long, bagel bakers realized an opportunity to sell directly to the consumer, rather than relying on restaurants to sell their goods. Home delivery was everywhere in the early part of the twentieth century, and before long, bagel peddlers were part of the fabric of these communities. Bagels were baked early in the morning and delivered directly to Brooklyn homes by Bagel Boys, just as they had been in Warsaw. However, as bagel shops proliferated and allowed the business-to-consumer model to flourish without incurring delivery costs, home deliveries of bagels began to decline.

There remained some outliers. Beginning in 1961 a synagogue in Chicago offered a Lox Box delivery containing breakfast for a family of four, to raise money for The City of Hope, an organization that helps with medical costs for Jewish community members in need. Synagogues and Jewish organizations around Chicago soon got in on the idea. Stories report on hours of debate, Talmudic in nature, about the contents of these boxes—especially whether or not tomatoes and cucumbers should be included. Over time, the original purpose of the boxes may have muddied, but for Jews who grew up in Chicago and its suburbs, Lox Boxes hold a near and dear place in their hearts.

Zingerman's in Ann Arbor, Michigan, didn't open until 1978, but quickly established itself as the region's mecca of deli food, including bagels. In fact, there was a time when your birthday at Zingerman's meant a free half-dozen bagels.

Since 2008, when small batch "makers" started opening craft businesses following the economic collapse, bagel bakeries have popped up everywhere. Like craft beer brewing and salumi making, bagel baking is an art to be perfected. Because the bagel business requires so few ingredients and very little special equipment, it's an easier entry point for many young entrepreneurs than a restaurant or bakery is. If a bagel bakery opens in your town, please give them your support. There's a long tradition of bagels, this nearly ancient bread from the Old Country that has become, somehow, a quintessentially American breakfast.

BAGEL TECHNIQUES

Step 1

MIXING

Before we talk about mixing the dough, allow me to preach the gospel of A Scale in Every Kitchen (see Kitchen Scale, page 23). A good kitchen scale provides precision, and that means every bagel you make can be as good as the previous one, consistently. But here is the real reason I love a scale: All of the ingredients for a basic bagel—flour, water, yeast, sweetener, salt—are added to the bowl at once. Using a scale means that there are no additional bowls or measuring cups to wash. While I have offered recipe weights for flour, water, and sweeteners, I prefer to use a measuring spoon for the small amounts of yeast and salt. My scale is not that precise. At the end of the mixing, there will be one bowl, the dough hook, one measuring spoon, and whatever I use to scrape down the bowl. I'll do anything to avoid dishes.

Mixing bagels takes a long time and a lot of strength, whether by hand or by machine. This a very stiff dough. I've made it by hand only a few times; it's much easier to set the timer and stand by while the mixer does the work.

Making bagel dough will tax a stand mixer (see page 23). Be aware of the strain making bagels will put on your equipment, and if you plan on starting a side hustle as a bagel baker, consider investing in a commercial-grade mixer.

For most classic bagel recipes, I start with the five essential elements (see page 19) weighed into the bowl of my stand mixer fitted with the dough hook. When I incorporate add-ins like fruit, nuts, or cheese, it's best to stir them in after the first rest (see Autolyse, following). Just about 7 minutes of machine-kneading and the dough is ready to be formed into bagels. It's a long stretch and it's really noisy but resist the urge to step away, as the mixer may hop and bump across the counter when you're not looking.

The following bagel recipes are written to be made in a stand mixer, but the dough can also be mixed and kneaded by hand. If you decide to make the dough by hand, be prepared for 20 minutes of solid kneading. Maybe a strong friend will help out.

Autolyse

Many years ago, I read a bread recipe with the instruction "Mix the ingredients and let them rest for a few minutes before a vigorous knead." This has proven to be one of the most useful pieces of kitchen wisdom I've ever tucked away.

Whenever I make any type of bread or yeasted dough, I use the mixer's dough hook to just combine the ingredients, ensuring there are no pockets of flour remaining and the dough is thoroughly combined, and then I stop and wait. I cover the bowl of the mixer with a clean tea towel and rest the dough for about 20 minutes, no more. (I like to use this time to do a quick cleanup or line the baking sheets.) This extra step of resting the dough after the ingredients are combined is called *autolyse*. It gives the flour time to absorb any liquids and lets the gluten rest before kneading. The result is a breezy knead and a smooth, bouncy dough. Any add-ins like raisins or nuts should go in after the autolyse.

Try this technique with all your yeasted bread baking. (You're welcome.)

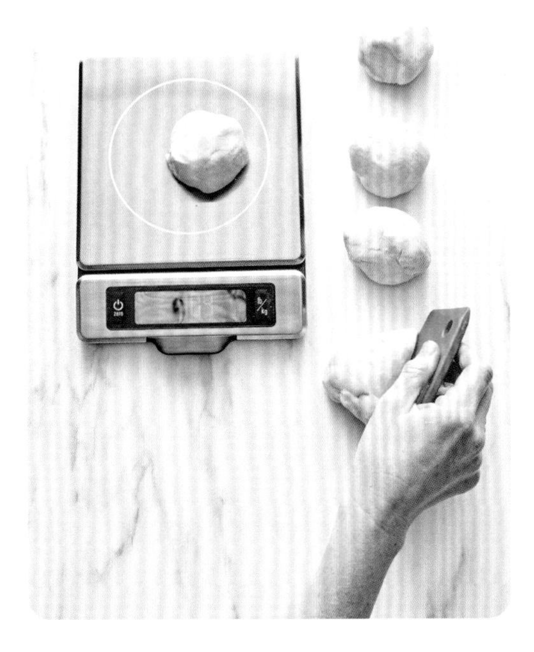

Step 2

SHAPING

My first attempts forming a bagel were comical. I ended up with so many bagels with no hole, only a vague dimple. It takes practice to make round bagels with a chewy crust and a bigger, better center hole. Forming bagels is not an ability you are born with—it's a skill both learned and honed. I worked to achieve bagel zen but, even still, the bagels do not slide off my fingers as perfect round rings. Do not get discouraged! Every bagel baked at home is delicious, even the homely ones. Bagel making definitely gets easier with practice.

Do not flour the work surface unless you're making The Bialy or The Pletzel (pages 67 and 63). This may seem *counter*intuitive (ha!), because so often when baking, we begin by dusting the work surface to keep the dough from sticking. In the case of bagels, a little friction is a good thing. Rolling the bagels on a clean, smooth surface builds a tension that will tighten the exterior shell and create the classic shiny crust.

Scoop the dough onto the work surface, then divide and weigh out the portions (the weight will depend on the type of bagel dough—refer to the recipe). Return to the first portion you weighed and flatten it into a disk, then lift and pull in the edges toward the center to form a ball. Place it seam-side down and roll the ball under your cupped palm to form a snug, smooth exterior. Repeat with the remaining portions, working in the same order in which they were weighed.

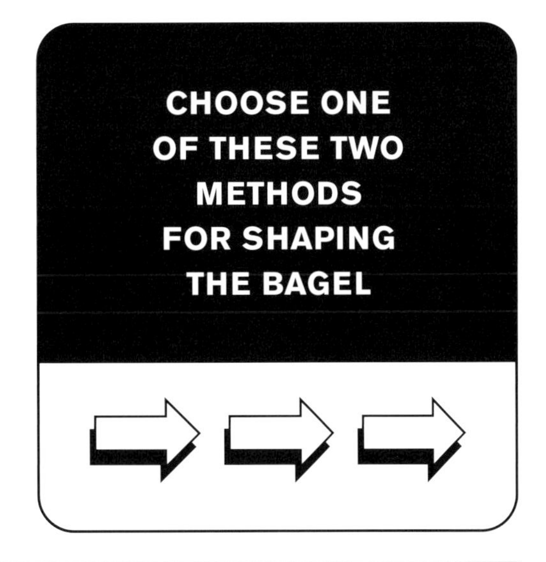

METHOD NO. 1

Roll 'Em

Starting with the first dough ball, form a 9 in [23 cm] rope by rolling and pressing your flattened palms from the center of the dough outward. Try to keep the rope an even thickness and blunt throughout—avoid tapering the ends. Next, form the rope into a ring by overlapping the ends and firmly pinching the seam. Place the bagel over four fingers and roll the dough at the seam forward and back along the counter, gently rotating the bagel without flattening, to tighten and smooth it. Put the thumb and forefinger of each hand into the center hole and stretch the bagel out. It will bounce back as it sits, so an exaggerated center hole is a good thing at this juncture.

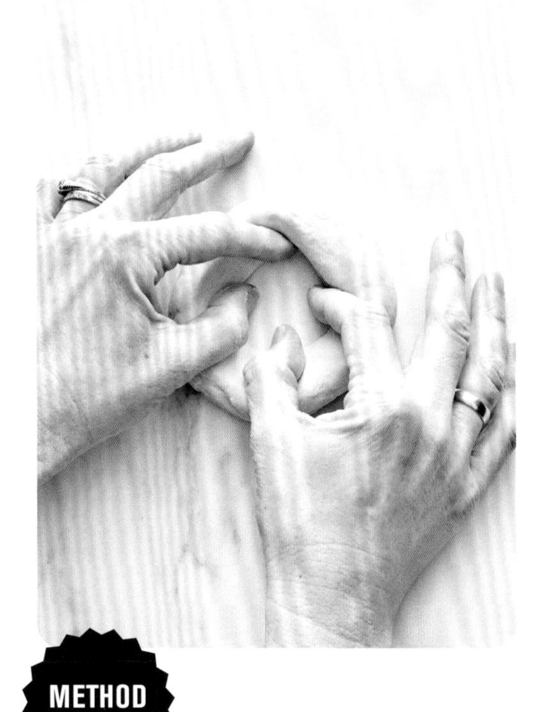

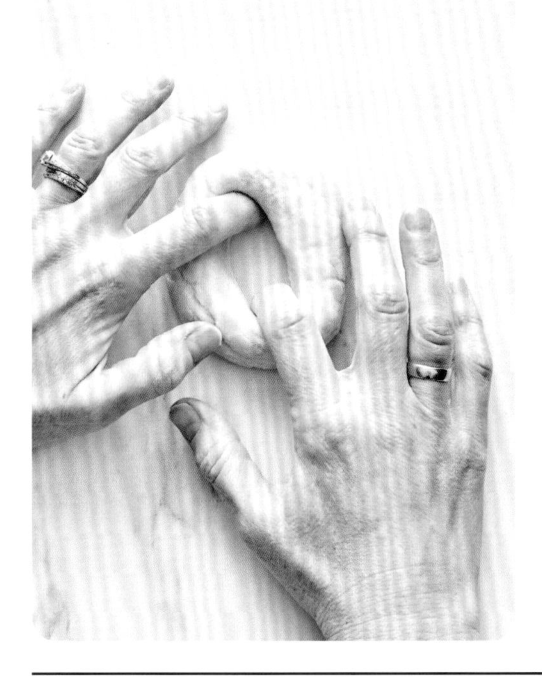

METHOD NO. 2

Poke 'Em

Start with the first dough ball and poke a thumb through the center to create a hole. Insert your two index fingers into the bagel's hole and rotate them around each other, stretching the bagel and expanding the hole to form a round bagel. Next, put the thumb and forefinger of each hand into the center hole to stretch the bagel out. It will bounce back as it sits, so an exaggerated center hole is a good thing at this juncture.

Once all the bagels are shaped, return to each to poke, pinch, scooch, and otherwise improve their form.

Mini Bagels

I hate to be Ms. Obvious here, but smaller portions of any of the following bagel recipes will make a mini bagel. Each should weigh, before baking, anywhere from 55 to 70 g [2 to 2½ oz], or half the unbaked weight of a full-size bagel. They will be an ideal tiny bagel for a brunch where people may want the chance to try different flavors or different schmears.

But that's not their only purpose. When I was growing up in Pittsburgh, Bagel Land always had a bag of mini bagels near the register for new moms. Turns out, a frozen mini bagel works great for teething babies!

Step 3

PROOFING

When it comes to proofing, bagels are the trickiest of any of the yeast-risen breads I've worked with. The combination of high-protein flour and plenty of sweetener makes them expand really fast. Incredibly fast. Before-your-eyes fast. Note that doubling in size might seem to make them ready for the oven, but their flavor will be flat unless given enough time to rise. A good bagel needs a slow, cold rise to develop its distinctive, tangy taste. Keep in mind that a cold rise doesn't stop the proofing, only slows it.

Once shaped, place the bagels on a baking sheet lined with a cornmeal-dusted piece of parchment (the cornmeal will keep the bagels from sticking as they proof). The baking sheet you use for proofing needs to be able to fit in your refrigerator; I fit six bagels on a quarter sheet pan (9 by 13 in [23 by 33 cm], and shallow, just 1 in [2.5 cm] deep). Cover the baking sheet and refrigerate the bagels. A piece of plastic wrap might stick to the unbaked bagels, so lightly coat the underside with cooking spray. Some baking sheets are available with snap-on covers and therefore don't require the plastic wrap. I find they are ideal for the overnight proof.

After a lot of testing, I have found that bagels need at least 8 hours and no more than 14 hours to proof after they go into the refrigerator, giving you a 6-hour window to work with. The sweet spot for proofing is 11 hours, so bagels formed after dinner will be ready for baking before breakfast. Unless making Montreal bagels, there is no way around this long cold rise, so try to time things out and plan accordingly.

Step 4

BOILING

By definition, bagels are boiled right before baking. Boiling is responsible for the crackly exterior and contributes to the shine on the crust. However, there are two schools of thought on the water bath: sweetened and unsweetened.

Montreal-style bagels are always boiled in water sweetened with honey or barley malt. Some New York bagels are bathed in sweetened water

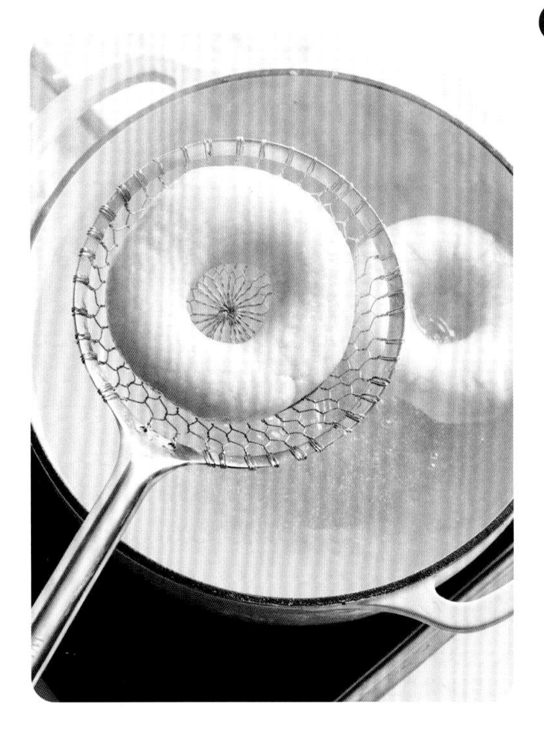

and some are not. I prefer to use an unsweetened water bath. It requires far less sweetener and avoids a sticky mess on baking day.

Before you begin boiling your bagels, get out a piece of parchment for the bagels to bake on. Ideally, you'll want to stage it on a pizza peel, a large cutting board, or a baking sheet flipped over. We're looking for a large, flat surface from which the parchment, covered with bagels, can slide into the oven unencumbered.

Always give the bagels time to shake off the chill of the refrigerator before boiling, no more than the few minutes needed to bring the water to a boil and preheat the oven.

Fill a deep, large pot with water and bring it to a boil; a 5 qt [4.7 L] Dutch oven works for two or three bagels at a time and heats up relatively quickly. When the water is boiling vigorously, lift the bagels one at a time from the proofing sheet. Use your fingers and be gentle, making every effort not to deflate them. If they stick, work slowly to liberate them and remember to use more cornmeal next time. If they've stuck to each other, use kitchen scissors to cut them apart.

Carefully drop the bagels into the boiling water; they should bob happily on the surface. If they sink, they may be under-proofed. A slightly under-proofed bagel might sink and then rise within 15 to 30 seconds; those will bake up just fine, if a little chewier than a properly proofed bagel. If the bagels remain on the bottom of the pot, they have not proofed for enough time or the yeast was spoiled. Don't bother baking them. If there are still bagels on the baking sheet, let them sit out at room temperature until they rise and puff up, about 30 minutes, and try again.

Alternatively, an over-proofed bagel will feel light as air when lifted into the water bath. It will float and bob along the surface, then deflate within a minute or two when removed from the water bath. An over-proofed bagel may reinflate in the oven, but, more frequently, it flattens and stays that way. It's still absolutely edible: Just rebrand it The Flagel (page 53), and enjoy its chewy nature.

When the bagels are in the water, use a spider or a wide slotted spoon to submerge and flip them over and over. They should spend about 60 to 90 seconds total in the boiling water, continuously being dunked and flipped. Small blisters may appear on the surface of the bagels. Fish the bagels out one at a time and either dunk them in the chosen toppings (see Getting the Seeds to Stick, page 48) or place them on the waiting parchment paper, making sure the side that had been sitting in the cornmeal remains down.

Bake the bagels as soon as possible after boiling or they may deflate—particularly if they are over-proofed.

Step 5

BAKING

Home bagel bakers must get their home ovens to emulate the power and ferocity of a blistering-hot deck oven. Bagels require high heat to puff, crisp, and get glossy. Really high heat. The struggle is real.

One way to achieve this power is to bake the bagels on a flat, preheated surface (not on a baking sheet—the sides of the sheet pan absorb too much heat to allow the edges of the bagels to crisp). I am a fan of the Baking Steel (see Tools of the Trade, page 25), a 15 lb [6.8 kg] slab of steel. Heating right along with the oven, the Baking Steel is screaming hot by the time I slide the bagels in. With a hot surface, the bagels bake on the bottom and sides as efficiently as they are baked on the top. The same quality can be achieved with a pizza stone and, to a lesser degree, with an inverted baking sheet left in the oven as the oven preheats. It will never get as hot as the Baking Steel or a pizza stone, but it's better to bake *on* a baking sheet than *in* one.

Ovens are sneaky, and the temperature they show on the dial may not be the true temperature inside. If your bagel baking is struggling, step back for a minute and be an oven detective.

The first step is to check the oven temperature with a thermometer. Oven thermometers are available everywhere, even the gadget aisle at the grocery store. Set the oven to 350°F [180°C] and check the thermometer. Now, increase the temperature by 25°F [15°C] and continue to check the oven thermometer against the oven's temperature on the dial. If you're on target, great. If not, either adjust the recipe to match the oven, or have the oven professionally calibrated.

Now, figure out if the oven is heating evenly. The wonderful, witty, generous cookbook author and teacher Nathalie Dupree taught me a great trick: Use a loaf of inexpensive sliced white bread as a diagnostic tool. Remove the center oven rack and heat the oven to 350°F [180°C]. Arrange the bread slices, touching side by side, flat on the oven rack, taking up every inch of space. When the oven reaches temperature, slide the rack of bread in and turn on the oven light. Watch it like a hawk; don't take your eyes off this experiment. Are the bread slices getting browned evenly or are the ones on one side burning while the ones on the other side are still pale? If the oven is heating unevenly, adjust the placement of the bagels to accommodate, or call for a repair.

Timing the Bake

I attempted a few different ways to bring bagels to the breakfast table without getting up at 4 a.m. or waiting until noon for breakfast. In time, I identified precisely the correct rhythm to boil and bake a breakfast of bagels in about an hour, counting from the time I wake up in the morning, put the coffee on, preheat the oven, and bring a pot of water to boil. It became an easy rhythm and bagels were soon a regular breakfast item as I honed my rolling and shaping skills.

Here's my recommendation: The night before, between 7 p.m. and 9 p.m., mix and shape the bagels and put the covered baking sheet in the refrigerator. It takes only about 20 minutes and (if you weigh ingredients) leaves only a bowl, dough hook, measuring spoon, bench scraper, and countertop to clean.

The next morning, heat the oven (with the Baking Steel in place), get a large pot of water boiling, and remove the bagels from the refrigerator. In my kitchen, heating the oven and bringing the water to a boil takes 20 to 25 minutes, so I have time to make coffee and let the dogs out. Boil the bagels, sprinkle on any toppings, and slide them into the oven. They're ready in 16 minutes, just enough time for a shower.

Bagel Baking at High Altitudes

At 3,500 ft [1,067 m] or more above sea level, bagel baking becomes a little challenging. Here are some adjustments you'll need to make to ensure your bagels bake properly and rise evenly.

- Increase the **oven temperature** from 450°F to 475°F [230°C to 245°C] . Decrease the **baking time** for most bagels from 16 minutes to 12 minutes. Use visual cues.
- Increase the **flour** by 1 Tbsp at 3,500 ft [1,067 m] above sea level and another 1 Tbsp for every 1,500 ft [457 m] above 3,500.
- Increase the **liquid** by 1 Tbsp at 3,500 ft [1,067 m] above sea level and another 1 Tbsp for every 1,000 ft [305 m].
- Decrease the **yeast** at over 3,500 ft [1,067 m] above sea level, from 1 Tbsp to 2¼ tsp.
- Expect a **shorter rise time**, even when refrigerated; proof no more than 11 hours. Use visual cues.

Step 6

SLICING

Or How to Slice a Bagel and Avoid Sunday Morning in the Emergency Room

Considering how challenging it can be to slice a bagel, it's not surprising that quite a few people end up in the hospital with bagel-specific injuries. I sport a faint scar on my left hand between thumb and first finger, so I feel qualified to speak to this topic.

Always use a serrated knife to slice a bagel, never a straight-edged knife, no matter how sharp. The serration works like a crosscut saw and not only is it a better way to cut any bread without smashing the crumb, but the toothy blade is less likely to slip across the crust and land in your hand. There are countertop bagel slicers on the market, both plastic and metal, that fit the bagel vertically, holding it steady as the guillotine knife passes through. Because they use a straight-edged knife, I am no fan.

Follow the deli guy's lead: Instead of holding the bagel in one hand as you cut downward, place the bagel flat on your work surface with one hand on the top to steady it. Carefully slice at the bagel's horizontal midway point, from one side to the other. Tip the bagel up to make the final cut through.

Stale bagels are harder to slice than fresh ones.

Never try to cut a frozen bagel. Instead, heat that bagel in a 350°F [180°C] oven for 10 to 12 minutes before slicing.

Step 7

STORING

After I bake bagels, I leave them on the counter either sitting on the wire rack or, once entirely cooled, in a bowl with a clean tea towel draped over the top. They will stay fresh for about 4 hours before they must be stored.

Properly sealed, bagels will last for 3 months in the freezer. Alternatively, wrap bagels in a bread bag and leave them out on the kitchen counter. Do not refrigerate them. Enjoy the bagels for 2 or 3 days, split and toasted, before they turn stale. Turn stale bagels into Bagel Chips (see following).

Plastic bread bags are available online and can be less expensive than zip-top bags, especially when you make bread or bagels regularly. They are handy when giving a gift of bagels too. Fabric bread bags and beeswax wrappers are a green alternative to all that plastic. And a bread box is the old-fashioned, perfectly sensible, counter-hogging vessel I love the most. Some households use the microwave as a substitute bread box, but it's not quite the same.

Bex Orris, who teaches bagel baking in Asheville, North Carolina, has very strong feelings about storage. In their mind, the bagel "comes with a protective shell." They recommend

freezing bagels after 4 hours and reheating them in a preheated 350°F [180°C] oven for 10 to 12 minutes. At that point, Bex says the bagels "are as near to freshly made as you can get" and can be sliced and enjoyed without toasting. They rail against slicing before freezing, remarking that once the bagel is cut, it starts to dry out. And in the cool, dry environment of a refrigerator or freezer, it will continue to dry out even more.

Bagel Chips

To make bagel chips, use a serrated knife to remove just the exterior crust from the top and bottom of the bagel. Slice the bagel into three thin rounds of equal width. Place the bagel pieces on a baking sheet and brush with butter, olive oil, bacon fat, or schmaltz. Sprinkle with seeds, spices, or grated cheese and bake in a preheated 325°F [165°C] oven for 12 minutes or until crisp. Cool and store in an airtight container for up to 5 days.

GEDEMPTE

TROUBLESHOOTING

Why is my bagel flat and deflated?

Either that bagel spent too long proofing in the refrigerator or it was boiled too long. It's also possible that the bagel did not come to room temperature before boiling. If you remove the bagels from the refrigerator before starting the boiling water or preheating the oven, by the time the water is ready, the chill will be gone from the bagels.

How will I know my bagel is ready to bake?

Bagels should nearly double in size from first shaping to boiling. They should feel light in the hand but not delicate or prone to deflation.

Why are my bagels dense?

Either they are under-proofed (see Proofing, page 36) or your yeast is old or expired.

Are there any tricks to knowing the bagel is properly proofed?

To test the proof, set aside a small nugget of dough while forming the bagels and place it on the baking sheet to proof with the bagels. Before boiling, see whether the nugget of dough floats in the boiling water. If it sinks and does not rise to the surface in about 30 seconds, those bagels need more resting time on the counter.

Can the bagel recipes in this book be doubled?

Yes. It's easy to double the recipe, and using a kitchen scale will make that effort successful. However, more dough will work the mixer even harder, so don't do it often unless you have a behemoth of a machine.

Is there a faster way to make a bagel?

Montreal bagels do not require a slow overnight rise. And they're delicious. (It is possible to mix and shape New York bagels and allow them to proof on the counter. In about an hour, they will be ready to bake but the flavor will be flat.)

The proofed bagels stuck to the parchment-lined baking sheet and I couldn't get them off without squishing them.

You forgot the cornmeal. Admit it—we've all done it. You'll love this handy trick I learned from Buttercream Bakeshop owner Tiffany MacIsaac: Use scissors to snip the parchment around the bagel into a square or rhombus or whatever shape you can. Use a large spatula to lift the bagel on its paper raft and lower it into the boiling water. The paper will float away; discard it and proceed with the bagel boiling.

THE NEW YORK BAGEL

MAKES 6

- 3 TBSP CORNMEAL, FOR DUSTING
- 420 G [3½ CUPS] HIGH-GLUTEN FLOUR (SEE FLOUR, PAGE 19, FOR SUBSTITUTIONS)
- 225 G [1 CUP] WATER
- 21 G [1 TBSP] BARLEY MALT SYRUP, MAPLE SYRUP, OR HONEY
- 1½ TSP KOSHER SALT
- 1 TSP INSTANT YEAST
- TOPPINGS, OPTIONAL (SEE GETTING THE SEEDS TO STICK, PAGE 48)

IT'S NOT ABOUT THE WATER, but it is about the flour. High-gluten flour, sometimes called high-protein flour, is critical to produce the tight exterior that bakes into the signature crisp crust of this classic style (see Tachlis, page 18). Expect a shiny, light, chewy, crackly, slightly sweet bagel, ready for a schmear. This is the quintessential New York bagel, even when it's baked in a kitchen far from the city's boroughs.

1 Line a baking sheet with parchment paper and scatter the cornmeal evenly across the paper. Set aside.

2 Place the bowl of a stand mixer on a kitchen scale and tare the weight to zero. Measure in the flour, water, barley malt syrup, salt, and yeast. Place the bowl back on the mixer and fit it with the dough hook. On low speed, mix the ingredients together until there are no dry patches of flour showing (see Mixing, page 32).

3 Stop to scrape down the sides of the bowl and increase the speed to medium. Mix until the sides of the bowl are nearly clean, 2 to 3 minutes. The dough may seem dry. Cover the bowl with a clean tea towel and let the dough rest for 20 minutes to allow the flour to hydrate evenly.

4 Uncover the bowl, turn the mixer speed back to medium, and let it run for 7 full minutes, until the dough is smooth and satiny and the sides of the bowl are clean. Watch the mixer at all times, as it might hop across the counter; the dough will be stiff and strong.

5 Scrape the dough onto a clean, unfloured work surface and give it five or six kneads. Divide the dough into six equal pieces, each weighing 110 g [just under 4 oz]. Shape the bagels (see Shaping, page 33) and place them on the prepared baking sheet. Cover the baking sheet tightly with plastic wrap that has been lightly coated with cooking spray and refrigerate overnight, or for at least 8 hours and no more than 14 hours (see Proofing, page 36). CONT'D

6 When ready to boil and bake, remove the bagels from the refrigerator and uncover, allowing them to come to room temperature while the oven heats and the water boils (see Timing the Bake, page 38). Place a pizza stone, Baking Steel, or inverted baking sheet on the oven's center rack and set the oven to its highest temperature, 450°F to 500°F [230°C to 260°C] in most home appliances (see Baking, page 38). Heat the oven for at least 30 minutes.

7 In the meantime, fill a 5 qt [4.7 L] or larger pot with water and bring it to a hard boil (see Boiling, page 36). Place a 9 by 13 in [23 by 33 cm] piece of parchment on a pizza peel, large cutting board, or an inverted baking sheet. (You need to be able to easily slide the bagel-laden parchment paper from this surface into the oven.)

8 The bagels should be slightly puffed from their overnight rise. Gently lift one at a time, brushing away any excess cornmeal, and drop it into the boiling water. Repeat with another one or two bagels only if they fit in the pot without crowding. Using a slotted spoon or spider, flip the bagels over and over in the water until very slightly puffed and shiny, about 60 seconds and no more than 90 seconds. Small blisters may appear on the surface.

9 Remove the bagels one by one and place cornmeal-side down on the parchment paper on the pizza peel. Sprinkle with any desired toppings while the bagels are still damp. Repeat with the remaining bagels; six bagels will fit snugly on the parchment paper without touching.

10 Lower the oven temperature to 450°F [230°C]. Slide the parchment paper with the bagels directly onto the hot surface in the oven and bake until deeply golden brown and shiny, 12 to 16 minutes (see Baking, page 38). To remove the bagels from the oven, slide the parchment paper right onto the peel. Transfer on their paper to a wire rack to cool.

11 As tempting as it is to grab the hot bagels immediately, allow them to cool slightly before eating. Eat within 4 hours or store (see Storing, page 40).

THE MONTREAL BAGEL

MAKES 6

For the bagels

- 3 TBSP CORNMEAL, FOR DUSTING
- 360 G [3 CUPS] ALL-PURPOSE FLOUR
- 175 G [¾ CUP] WATER
- 42 G [2 TBSP] LIGHT CLOVER OR WILDFLOWER HONEY
- 15 G [2 TBSP] NEUTRAL OIL, LIKE CANOLA
- 1 TSP KOSHER SALT
- ½ TSP INSTANT YEAST

For the topping

- 71 G [½ CUP] SESAME SEEDS OR ALL-DRESSED SPICE (PAGE 49), OPTIONAL

For the water bath

- 3 QT [2.8 L] WATER
- 85 G [¼ CUP] LIGHT CLOVER OR WILDFLOWER HONEY

AMERICA'S NEIGHBORS to the north make a very different bagel. Montreal bagels are smaller and flatter, there is no tight exterior crust, and the interior crumb is more cakey than chewy. They tend to be craggy, uneven, and a little homely, and are most often thickly covered with sesame seeds on both the top and bottom. They do not require an overnight rise, so this is the bagel to make when you wake up craving a freshly baked bagel for brunch. Montreal bagels are always boiled in sweetened water and baked in a wood oven. Sadly, few of us have a wood-fired oven at home, so this recipe is my best approximation. I think they are ideal for bagel sandwiches and a sweet, tender addition to a bagel brunch at which many people will rhapsodize with stories of trips to St-Viateur and Fairmount bagel bakeries.

1 To make the bagels, line a baking sheet with parchment paper and scatter the cornmeal evenly across the paper. Set aside.

2 Place the bowl of a stand mixer on a kitchen scale and tare the weight to zero. Measure in the flour, water, honey, oil, salt, and yeast. Place the bowl back on the stand mixer and fit it with the dough hook. On low speed, mix the ingredients together until there are no dry patches of flour showing (see Mixing, page 32). **CONT'D**

3 Stop to scrape down the sides of the bowl and increase the speed to medium. Mix until the sides of the bowl are nearly clean, 2 to 3 minutes. The dough may seem dry. Cover the bowl with a clean tea towel and let the dough rest for 10 minutes to allow the flour to hydrate evenly.

4 Uncover the bowl, turn the mixer speed to medium, and let it run for 5 full minutes, until the dough is smooth and satiny and the sides of the bowl are clean.

5 Scrape the dough onto a clean, unfloured work surface and give it five or six kneads. Divide the dough into six equal pieces, each weighing about 97 g [3⅜ oz]. Shape the bagels using the Poke 'Em method (see Shaping, page 35) and stretch the center hole with the thumbs and forefingers of both hands. These will be rougher looking than New York bagels (page 43), uneven and bumpy. One at a time, form and place the bagels on the prepared baking sheet. Cover the baking sheet tightly with plastic wrap that has been lightly coated with cooking spray and set in a cool place to rise until slightly puffed, about 1 hour.

6 About 15 minutes before the rise is over, place a pizza stone, Baking Steel, or inverted baking sheet on the oven's center rack and set the oven to 400°F [200°C].

7 To prepare the topping, pour the seeds, if using, into a pie pan or another shallow dish.

8 To make the water bath, add the water and honey to a 5 qt [4.7 L] or larger pot and bring it to a hard boil (see Boiling, page 36). Place a 9 by 13 in [23 by 33 cm] piece of parchment on a pizza peel, large cutting board, or a baking sheet flipped over. (You need to be able to easily slide the bagel-laden parchment paper from this surface into the oven.)

9 The bagels will have risen to only about 50 percent more than their starting size. Gently lift one at a time, brushing away any excess cornmeal, and drop it into the boiling water. Repeat with another one or two bagels only if they fit in the pot without crowding. Using a slotted spoon or spider, flip the bagels over and over in the water until very slightly puffed, about 60 seconds and no more than 90 seconds.

10 Transfer each bagel to the pan of seeds, using a chopstick to flip the bagel so the seeds stick to both sides, then move it to the parchment paper on the pizza peel. Repeat with the remaining bagels; six bagels will fit snugly on the parchment paper without touching.

11 Slide the parchment paper with the bagels directly onto the hot surface in the oven and bake until lightly golden brown and shiny, 16 to 20 minutes (see Baking, page 38). To remove the bagels from the oven, slide the parchment paper right onto the peel. Transfer on their paper to a wire rack to cool.

12 As tempting as it is to grab the hot bagels immediately, allow them to cool slightly before eating. Eat within 4 hours or store (see Storing, page 40).

HOT!

GETTING THE SEEDS TO STICK

Bagels benefit from a tasty sprinkling of seeds, but every bagel baker struggles with keeping them in place.

I've tried every method: I've dipped the boiled bagels in egg white and then in seeds, which makes the seeds stick but changes the outside crust. I read about a tapioca starch slurry in a modernist book, but that was just too fussy and involved too much equipment.

It was only when I stopped worrying about wasting seeds and began buying in large quantities at an international grocer that I found a decent solution. I transfer each wet bagel straight from the water bath into a deep bowlful of the seeds. Then I flip the bagel over to coat both sides. To transfer it back to the waiting parchment, I quickly lift the bagel with a chopstick poked through the hole.

After coating the bagels, you'll be left with a bowl of damp seeds. They will mold unless dried entirely before storing. Damp seeds can be spread on a baking sheet and dried in a 225°F [110°C] oven, then reused for the next batch.

Here's the reality: I don't bother with a deep bowl of seeds when making six bagels for the two of us. I only do that when I'm making bagels for a big group. In real life, I sprinkle the seeds over the top of the bagels when they're still wet from the boiling water bath for a consistent coating on the top surface only.

Sadly, once baked, some seeds just don't stick. When they come off on your plate, scoop them up and sprinkle them over the schmear. That's what schmear is for.

SESAME SEEDS

While it's possible to purchase sesame seeds already toasted, they may turn bitter when retoasted on a baking bagel. Asian and Latin groceries sell bulk bags of raw sesame seeds. Always smell or taste the seeds first to be certain they are not rancid. Store sesame seeds in the freezer for up to 3 months.

POPPY SEEDS

Be generous with poppy seeds in every application. They are both flavorful and beautiful. Sniff poppy seeds before using to make sure they haven't turned rancid; it happens very quickly. Purchase in quantity for a better value, and store in the freezer for up to 3 months.

SALT

Salt bagels are best when the crystals are large and visible. I like to use pretzel salt because it doesn't dissolve when it comes into contact with a wet bagel, but Maldon and other large crystal salts will also work.

ONION

Flecks of dehydrated onion across the surface of a bagel deliver powerful flavor and aroma, but they typically get a bit burnt on the edges. Large flakes of onion will fare better than small ones. I've tried soaking the dehydrated onions first, to avoid the burn, but ended up with soggy onions. I love Litehouse brand freeze-dried red onions, but they're a little spendy.

GARLIC

Garlic is similar to onions: When those topping bits blacken in the oven, they turn a bagel bitter and miserable. Rehydrating dried garlic will only give you a soggy bagel. Avoid the flaked garlic you find on the grocery spice aisle and look for freeze-dried garlic granules instead. I like the Litehouse brand for these as well.

KUMMELWECK

Kummelweck (or weck) combines equal parts caraway seed and coarse salt ground in a mortar and pestle and used as a sprinkle. Kummelweck brings out the rye flavor in a pumpernickel bagel nicely.

TOGARASHI

Togarashi, available commercially or made at home, is also known as Japanese Seven Spice Blend. I call it Japanese Everything Spice. It's typically a combination of chile peppers, Sichuan peppercorns, dried orange peel, black and white sesame seeds, ginger, poppy seeds, and nori seaweed. It's spicy and salty like seawater. I love the combination of orange and ginger and what it does to an egg bagel. Find Togarashi in the international aisle of your grocery store, at Asian markets, and online.

GOMASIO

Gomasio, also called seaweed salt, is a blend of unhulled sesame seeds, salt, and nori seaweed. It is a central flavoring in macrobiotic cooking. Try it in place of sesame seeds where it will add the nuanced flavor of the sea to the expected sesame flavor. Find gomasio in the health food or international aisle of your grocery store, at Asian markets, and online.

EVERYTHING SPICE (ALL-DRESSED SPICE)

It's called Everything Spice for a reason. It's got everything, so put in there what you like. This recipe is my basic combination, but sometimes I'll add fennel seed or crushed red pepper. Other times, I leave out the garlic and add charnushka (nigella) seeds. Some people love caraway in their everything bagels; others find caraway an offense against all bagels. In Montreal, it's called "All-Dressed" and never includes salt. This is only a guide, so create your own blend and make it all yours.

MAKES ABOUT ¼ CUP [38 G]

2 Tbsp poppy seeds

2 Tbsp sesame seeds, white, black, or both

1 Tbsp dehydrated onion

2 tsp kosher salt, pretzel salt, Maldon salt, or coarse fleur de sel

1 tsp freeze-dried garlic granules

In a small jar, mix together the poppy seeds, sesame seeds, onion, salt, and garlic. Cover and store in the refrigerator for 3 months.

Thank You—Come Again

THE PUMPERNICKEL BAGEL

MAKES 6

- 3 TBSP CORNMEAL, FOR DUSTING
- 320 G [2⅔ CUPS] HIGH-GLUTEN FLOUR (SEE FLOUR, PAGE 19 FOR SUBSTITUTIONS)
- 106 G [1 CUP] PUMPERNICKEL FLOUR (SEE PAGE 52)
- 225 G [1 CUP] WATER
- 21 G [1 TBSP] BARLEY MALT SYRUP, MAPLE SYRUP, OR HONEY
- 20 G [1 TBSP] UNSULFURED MOLASSES OR SORGHUM
- 5 G [1 TBSP] NATURAL COCOA POWDER
- 1½ TSP KOSHER SALT
- 1 TSP INSTANT YEAST
- TOPPINGS, OPTIONAL (SEE PAGE 48)

MY BROTHER, DAVID, rhapsodizes, even many decades later, about the warm pumpernickel bagel smeared with butter that was his afterschool snack for all of high school. Pumpernickel bagels are rare birds that deserve to be brought back from obscurity. The pumpernickel flour suppresses the crackly outer shell for a softer bagel more akin to an egg bagel, making them terrific sandwich bagels. Fancy them up with an Everything Spice topping (page 49) or make Pumpernickel Raisin Bagels (page 58). Or, twist the pumpernickel dough with plain bagel dough to make the showiest of all bagels—The Marble Bagel (page 55).

1 Line a baking sheet with parchment paper and scatter the cornmeal evenly across the paper. Set aside.

2 Place the bowl of a stand mixer on a kitchen scale and tare the weight to zero. Measure in the high-gluten and pumpernickel flours, water, barley malt syrup, molasses, cocoa powder, salt, and yeast. Place the bowl back on the mixer and fit it with the dough hook. On low speed, mix the ingredients together until there are no dry patches of flour showing (see Mixing, page 32).

3 Stop to scrape down the sides of the bowl and increase the speed to medium. Mix until the sides of the bowl are nearly clean, 2 to 3 minutes. The dough may seem dry. Cover the bowl with a clean tea towel and let the dough rest for 20 minutes to allow the flour to hydrate evenly.

4 Uncover the bowl, turn the mixer speed back to medium, and let it run for 7 full minutes, until the dough is smooth and satiny and the sides of the bowl are clean. Watch the mixer at all times, as it might hop across the counter; the dough will be stiff and strong. **CONT'D**

5 Scrape the dough onto a clean, unfloured work surface and give it five or six kneads. Divide the dough into six equal pieces, each weighing 115 g [about 4 oz]. Shape the bagels (see Shaping, page 33) and place them on the prepared baking sheet. Cover the baking sheet tightly with plastic wrap that has been lightly coated with cooking spray and refrigerate overnight, or for at least 8 hours and no more than 14 hours (see Proofing, page 36).

6 When ready to boil and bake, remove the bagels from the refrigerator and uncover, allowing them to come to room temperature while the oven heats and the water boils (see Timing the Bake, page 38). Place a pizza stone, Baking Steel, or inverted baking sheet on the oven's center rack and set the oven to its highest temperature, 450°F to 500°F [230°C to 260°C] in most home appliances (see Baking, page 38). Heat the oven for at least 30 minutes.

7 In the meantime, fill a 5 qt [4.7 L] or larger pot with water and bring it to a hard boil (see Boiling, page 36). Place a 9 by 13 in [23 by 33 cm] piece of parchment on a pizza peel, large cutting board, or an inverted baking sheet. (You need to be able to easily slide the bagel-laden parchment paper from this surface into the oven.)

8 The bagels should be slightly puffed from their overnight rise. Gently lift one at a time, brushing away any excess cornmeal, and drop it into the boiling water. Repeat with another one or two bagels only if they fit in the pot without crowding. Using a slotted spoon or spider, flip the bagels over and over in the water until very slightly puffed and shiny, about 60 seconds and no more than 90 seconds. Small blisters may appear on the surface.

9 Remove the bagels one by one and place cornmeal-side down on the parchment paper on the pizza peel. Sprinkle with any desired toppings while the bagels are still damp. Repeat with the remaining bagels; six bagels will fit snugly on the parchment paper without touching.

10 Lower the oven heat to 450°F [230°C]. Slide the parchment paper with bagels directly onto the hot surface in the oven and bake until deep brown and shiny, 12 to 16 minutes (see Baking, page 38). To remove the bagels from the oven, slide the parchment paper right onto the peel. Transfer on their paper to a wire rack to cool.

11 As tempting as it is to grab the hot bagels immediately, allow them to cool slightly before eating. Eat within 4 hours or store (see Storing, page 40).

WHAT IS PUMPERNICKEL?

PUMPERNICKEL FLOUR
is milled from the whole rye berry, including the fiber, bran, and germ. It's dark and flavorful in a way no other rye flour is.

MY SISTER-IN-LAW CAROLA,
German by birth, was kind enough to research the etymology. The origins of the German word seem to be *pumper*, which refers to a digestive noise (ahem), and *nickel*, a coarse term for a country bumpkin. Further vernacular hijinks resulted in a nickname, the Devil's Fart.

AS FOR SUBSTITUTIONS,
some sources call for three parts dark rye flour plus one part whole-wheat flour to replicate the pumpernickel flavor. But to me, that combo falls short of the original. True pumpernickel flour is not difficult to source, and the rewards justify the effort.

HOT!

BAGELS AND THEIR MISHPOCHA

THE TURKISH SIMIT

An Istanbul treasure, the round, twisted, sesame-coated simit is, like the Jerusalem bagel, baked but not boiled. It may be the very first of the traditionally round breads with which the bagel shares some culinary DNA. After all, the simit is made with flour, water, yeast, salt, and molasses, identical to the Tachlis that make up a bagel.

ISRAEL'S JERUSALEM BAGEL

All across Jerusalem, there's a bagel that bears the city's name. The Jerusalem bagel is sold almost exclusively from street carts that ring the markets in the old city. Recently, some outlets in Los Angeles and Philadelphia have introduced Americans to this slightly sweet, bready cousin of the stiffer-shelled New York bagel. Oblong in shape, slightly flat, never boiled, and generously coated in sesame seeds, the Jerusalem bagel is served with labneh dusted with za'atar. Culinary historians suspect the Jerusalem bagel has its roots in the Turkish simit.

THE FLAGEL

Flagels—flattened bagels—first appeared in New York City sometime around 1990, according to a *Village Voice* article that was later disputed by the *New York Post.* All that really matters is that they exist. It's only speculation on my part, after making dozens of bagels myself, but I would bet that a baker had a proofing failure and accidentally created a flat bagel that failed to rise or was so over-proofed it couldn't hold up the domed crust. Marketing and rebranding took hold, and the flagel entered the zeitgeist. The moment coincided with a low-carb food phase, and somehow the flagel satisfied those dieters. Go figure.

All that aside, the flagel turns out to be an excellent sandwich bagel. It's easier to take a bite from a flagel sandwich, even with a generous filling (see Bagel Sandwiches and Salads, page 178).

To make a flagel intentionally, when the bagel is lifted from the boiling water bath, place it on the baking sheet and lightly roll over it with a rolling pin or press down gently with a flat palm to squish it, then coat with seeds, if desired. Proceed with baking as usual.

THE MARBLE BAGEL

MAKES 12

$\frac{2}{3}$ CUP [90 G] CORNMEAL, FOR DUSTING

1 RECIPE NEW YORK BAGEL, UNPROOFED DOUGH (PAGE 43)

1 RECIPE PUMPERNICKEL BAGEL, UNPROOFED DOUGH (PAGE 51)

TOPPINGS, OPTIONAL (SEE PAGE 48)

MARBLE BAGELS TWIST TOGETHER the best of both worlds, using the dough from both pumpernickel and classic New York bagels. Because you'll need to make two doughs before the marble bagels can be formed, work with one dough at a time, dividing, weighing, and rolling it into ropes. Cover and refrigerate those pieces while repeating the process. Once the ropes are twisted together, use the Roll 'Em method (see page 34) to do a final shaping.

1 Line two baking sheets with parchment paper and scatter half the cornmeal evenly over each one. Set aside.

2 Uncover and place the New York bagel dough on a clean, unfloured work surface. Divide the dough into twelve equal pieces, each about 55 g [2 oz]. Shape each portion into a ball, tightening the exterior by rolling it under your palm against the work surface. Starting with the first ball of dough, roll it into a rope about 9 in [23 cm] long. Repeat with the remaining pieces of dough. Cover and refrigerate the twelve ropes while repeating the process with the pumpernickel bagel dough.

3 Working with two ropes at a time, one New York and the other pumpernickel, twist them around each other three times. Pinch the two ropes together at the ends and then pinch those ends together to form a ring. Place the ring over four fingers on one hand and gently roll the seam along the counter to smooth the connection point. Place the thumb and forefinger of each hand in the bagel's hole and stretch it out to make a generous center opening.

4 As each bagel is shaped, place it on one of the prepared baking sheets and repeat with the remaining portions, placing six bagels on each baking sheet.

5 Cover the baking sheets tightly with plastic wrap that has been lightly coated with cooking spray. Refrigerate overnight, or for at least 8 hours and no more than 14 hours (see Proofing, page 36).

6 When ready to boil and bake, remove all twelve bagels from the refrigerator (you'll be baking in two separate batches of six) and uncover, allowing them to come to room temperature while the oven heats and the water boils (see Timing the Bake, page 38). Place a pizza stone, Baking Steel, or inverted baking sheet on the oven's center rack and set the oven to its highest temperature, 450°F to 500°F [230°C to 260°C] in most home appliances (see Baking, page 38). Heat the oven for at least 30 minutes. **CONT'D**

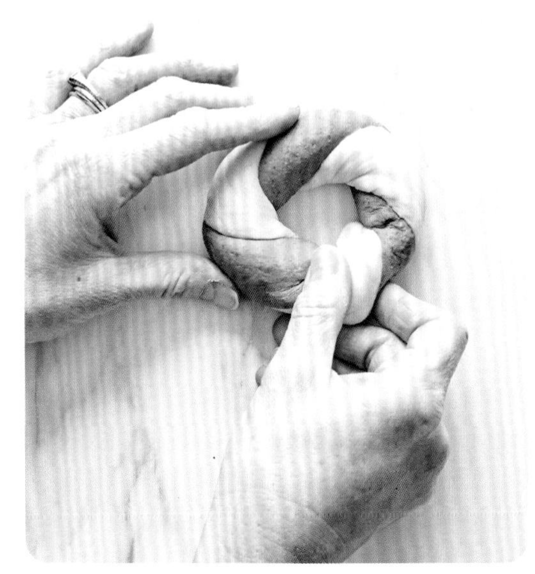

7 In the meantime, fill a 5 qt [4.7 L] or larger pot with water and bring it to a hard boil (see Boiling, page 36). Place a 9 by 13 in [23 by 33 cm] piece of parchment on a pizza peel, large cutting board, or an inverted baking sheet. (You need to be able to easily slide the bagel-laden parchment paper from this surface into the oven.)

8 The bagels will be slightly puffed from their overnight rise. Gently lift one at a time, brush away any cornmeal, and drop it into the boiling water. Repeat with another one or two bagels only if they fit in the pot without crowding. Using a slotted spoon or spider, flip the bagels over and over in the water until very slightly puffed and shiny, about 60 seconds and no more than 90 seconds. Small blisters may appear on the surface.

9 Remove the bagels one by one and place cornmeal-side down on the parchment paper on the pizza peel. Sprinkle with any desired toppings while the bagels are still damp. Repeat with the remaining bagels; six bagels will fit snugly on the parchment paper without touching.

10 Lower the oven heat to 450°F [230°C]. Slide the parchment paper with the bagels directly onto the hot surface in the oven and bake until deeply golden brown and shiny, 12 to 16 minutes (see Baking, page 38). To remove the bagels from the oven, slide the parchment paper right onto the peel. Transfer on their paper to a wire rack to cool. Repeat the boiling, baking, and cooling with the remaining six bagels.

11 As tempting as it is to grab the hot bagels immediately, allow them to cool slightly before eating. Eat within 4 hours or store (see Storing, page 40).

THE CINNAMON RAISIN BAGEL

MAKES 6

- 3 TBSP CORNMEAL, FOR DUSTING
- 45 G [1/3 CUP] SEEDLESS RAISINS (GOLDEN OR DARK), PLUMPED FOR 5 MINUTES IN BOILING WATER TO COVER
- 2 TBSP GRANULATED SUGAR
- 1 TSP GROUND CINNAMON
- 1/2 TSP NATURAL OR DUTCH-PROCESS COCOA POWDER
- 1/4 TSP GRATED NUTMEG
- 420 G [3 1/2 CUPS] HIGH-GLUTEN FLOUR (SEE FLOUR, PAGE 19, FOR SUBSTITUTIONS)
- 21 G [1 TBSP] BARLEY MALT SYRUP, MAPLE SYRUP, OR HONEY
- 1 1/2 TSP KOSHER SALT
- 1 1/4 TSP INSTANT YEAST

PEOPLE WHO LIKE A CINNAMON RAISIN BAGEL are going to love this aromatic rendition. The dough is scented with cinnamon, nutmeg, and a hint of cocoa. The raisins are plump and distributed throughout. If your raisins are huge, chop them into smaller pieces. For the raisin-averse, feel free to substitute other dried fruits—whole cherries and cranberries, or chopped figs, dates, apricots, or prunes, all work well, by weight. Be aware of the timing, though—the sugar and fruit will supercharge the yeast, so these bagels are prone to over-proofing.

1 Line a baking sheet with parchment paper and scatter the cornmeal evenly across the paper. Set aside.

2 Strain the plumped raisins, reserving the liquid. Pat the raisins dry and place in a small bowl. Sprinkle with the sugar, cinnamon, cocoa powder, and nutmeg. Set aside.

3 Add enough water to the reserved raisin water to weigh 225 g [1 cup].

4 Place the bowl of a stand mixer on a kitchen scale and tare the weight to zero. Measure in the flour, raisin water, barley malt syrup, salt, and yeast. Place the bowl back on the mixer and fit it with the dough hook. On low speed, mix the ingredients together until there are no dry patches of flour showing (see Mixing, page 32).

5 Stop to scrape down the sides of the bowl and increase the speed to medium. Mix until the sides of the bowl are nearly clean, 2 to 3 minutes. The dough may seem dry. Cover the bowl with a clean tea towel and let the dough rest for 20 minutes to allow the flour to hydrate evenly.

CONT'D

6 Uncover and remove the bowl from the mixer. Add the raisin mixture, using a stiff spatula or wooden spoon to fold it into the dough a few times. Return the bowl to the mixer base and turn the speed to low for 2 to 3 minutes to further incorporate the raisins. Stop to scrape down the sides of the bowl and push the dough off the hook.

7 Turn the mixer speed back to low, mixing until the ingredients are well incorporated, then increase the speed to medium and let it run for 7 full minutes, until the dough is smooth and the sides of the bowl are clean. Watch the mixer at all times, as it might hop across the counter; the dough will be stiff and strong.

8 Scrape the dough onto a clean, unfloured work surface and give it five or six kneads. Divide the dough into six equal pieces, each weighing 125 g [just under 4⅜ oz]. Shape the bagels (see Shaping, page 33) and place them on the prepared baking sheet. Cover the baking sheet tightly with plastic wrap that has been lightly coated with cooking spray and refrigerate overnight, or for at least 8 hours and no more than 12 hours (see Proofing, page 36).

9 When ready to boil and bake, remove the bagels from the refrigerator and uncover, allowing them to come to room temperature while the oven heats and the water boils (see Timing the Bake, page 38). Place a pizza stone, Baking Steel, or inverted baking sheet on the oven's center rack and set the oven to its highest temperature, 450°F to 500°F [230°C to 260°C] in most home appliances (see Baking, page 38). Heat the oven for at least 30 minutes.

10 In the meantime, fill a 5 qt [4.7 L] or larger pot with water and bring it to a hard boil (see Boiling, page 36). Place a 9 by 13 in [23 by 33 cm] piece of parchment on a pizza peel, large cutting board, or an inverted baking sheet. (You need to be able to easily slide the bagel-laden parchment paper from this surface into the oven.)

11 The bagels will be slightly puffed from their overnight rise. Gently lift one at a time, brush away any excess cornmeal, and drop it into the boiling water. Repeat with another one or two bagels only if they fit in the pot without crowding. Using a slotted spoon or spider, flip the bagels over and over in the water until very slightly puffed and shiny, about 60 seconds and no more than 90 seconds. Small blisters may appear on the surface.

12 Remove the bagels one by one and place cornmeal-side down on the parchment paper on the pizza peel. Repeat with the remaining bagels; six bagels will fit snugly on the parchment paper without touching.

13 Lower the oven temperature to 450°F [230°C]. Slide the parchment paper with the bagels directly onto the hot surface in the oven and bake until deeply golden brown and shiny, 12 to 16 minutes (see Baking, page 38). To remove the bagels from the oven, slide the parchment paper right onto the peel. Transfer on their paper to a wire rack to cool.

14 As tempting as it is to grab the hot bagels immediately, allow them to cool slightly before eating. Eat within 4 hours or store (see Storing, page 40).

VARIATION

THE PUMPERNICKEL RAISIN BAGEL

Substitute 106 g [1 cup] pumpernickel flour for an equal weight of high-gluten flour.

THE EGG BAGEL

MAKES 6

3 TBSP CORNMEAL, FOR DUSTING

420 G [3½ CUPS] HIGH-GLUTEN FLOUR (SEE FLOUR, PAGE 19, FOR SUBSTITUTIONS)

150 G [⅔ CUP] LUKEWARM WATER

1 LARGE EGG PLUS 1 LARGE EGG YOLK

42 G [2 TBSP] CLOVER OR WILDFLOWER HONEY

8 G [1 TBSP] NEUTRAL OIL, LIKE CANOLA

1½ TSP KOSHER SALT

1 TSP INSTANT YEAST

TOPPINGS, OPTIONAL (SEE PAGE 48)

WITH A SOFTER EXTERIOR and a more tender interior than a classic New York bagel, egg bagels in the United States are closer in flavor to the sweet Montreal bagel. I'll admit, even though it's my BFF's favorite bagel, the egg bagel's charms eluded me. Now that I've made them myself, I understand them better. They're like challah, but chewy; honeyed and beautifully yellow and, when toasted, a swath of peanut butter with a drizzle of even more honey makes them shine. Use fresh eggs with vibrantly colored yolks, and the bagels will look like sunshine.

1 Line a baking sheet with parchment paper and scatter the cornmeal evenly across the paper. Set aside.

2 Place the bowl of a stand mixer on a kitchen scale and tare the weight to zero. Measure in the flour, water, egg and yolk, honey, oil, salt, and yeast. Place the bowl back on the mixer and fit it with the dough hook. On low speed, mix the ingredients together until there are no dry patches of flour showing (see Mixing, page 32).

3 Stop to scrape down the sides of the bowl and increase the speed to medium. Mix until the sides of the bowl are nearly clean, 2 to 3 minutes. The dough may seem dry. Cover the bowl with a clean tea towel and let the dough rest for 20 minutes to allow the flour to hydrate evenly.

4 Uncover the bowl, turn the mixer speed back to medium, and let it run for 7 full minutes, until the dough is smooth and satiny and the sides of the bowl are clean. Watch the mixer at all times, as it might hop across the counter; the dough will be stiff and strong. **CONT'D**

5 Scrape the dough onto a clean, unfloured work surface and give it five or six kneads. Divide the dough into six equal pieces, each weighing about 135 g [4¾ oz]. Shape the bagels (see Shaping, page 33) and place them on the prepared baking sheet. Cover the baking sheet tightly with plastic wrap that has been lightly coated with cooking spray and refrigerate overnight, or for at least 8 hours and no more than 14 hours (see Proofing, page 36).

6 When ready to boil and bake, remove the bagels from the refrigerator and uncover, allowing them to come to room temperature while the oven heats and the water boils (see Timing the Bake, page 38). Place a pizza stone, Baking Steel, or inverted baking sheet on the oven's center rack and set the oven to its highest temperature, 450°F to 500°F [230°C to 260°C] in most home appliances (see Baking, page 38). Heat the oven for at least 30 minutes.

7 In the meantime, fill a 5 qt [4.7 L] or larger pot with water and bring it to a hard boil (see Boiling, page 36). Place a 9 by 13 in [23 by 33 cm] piece of parchment on a pizza peel, large cutting board, or an inverted baking sheet. (You need to be able to easily slide the bagel-laden parchment paper from this surface into the oven.)

8 The bagels should be slightly puffed from their overnight rise. Gently lift one at a time, brushing away any excess cornmeal, and drop it into the boiling water. Repeat with another one or two bagels only if they fit in the pot without crowding. Using a slotted spoon or spider, flip the bagels over and over in the water until very slightly puffed and shiny, about 60 seconds and no more than 90 seconds. Small blisters may appear on the surface.

9 Remove the bagels one by one and place cornmeal-side down on the parchment paper on the pizza peel. Sprinkle with any desired toppings while the bagels are still damp. Repeat with the remaining bagels; six bagels will fit snugly on the parchment without touching.

10 Lower the oven temperature to 450°F [230°C]. Slide the parchment paper with bagels directly onto the hot surface in the oven and bake until deeply golden, 12 to 16 minutes (see Baking, page 38). To remove the bagels from the oven, slide the parchment paper right onto the peel. Transfer on their paper to a wire rack to cool.

11 As tempting as it is to grab the hot bagels immediately, allow them to cool slightly before eating. Eat within 4 hours or store (see Storing, page 40).

THE PLETZEL

MAKES 1

For the pletzel

- 300 G [2½ CUPS] ALL-PURPOSE FLOUR, PLUS MORE FOR DUSTING
- 3 TBSP SCHMALTZ (SEE PAGE 64) OR OLIVE OIL, PLUS MORE FOR GREASING AND DRIZZLING
- 225 G [1 CUP] WATER
- 1½ TSP INSTANT YEAST
- 1½ TSP KOSHER SALT

For the topping

- 2 TBSP SCHMALTZ OR OLIVE OIL, PLUS MORE FOR BRUSHING
- 500 G [4 CUPS] THINLY SLICED YELLOW ONIONS (ABOUT 2 MEDIUM ONIONS SLICED INTO HALF-MOONS)
- ½ TSP KOSHER SALT
- 2 TBSP PLAIN DRIED BREAD CRUMBS
- ½ TSP FLAKY FINISHING SALT

THE PLETZEL (OR PLETSEL, PLETZLACH) or onion board is not very well known, but it should be. The pletzel is most similar to focaccia, with a dimpled surface on a yeasted dough. For onion lovers, it's topped with a filling similar to the topping on a bialy. For bread lovers, there's a tender crumb and squishy center that's the perfect foil to chewy, dense bagels. On a bread board for bagel brunch, it should be mandatory. Both the dough and the onion filling may be made up to 2 days in advance.

1 To make the pletzel, place the bowl of a stand mixer on a kitchen scale and tare the weight to zero. Measure in half of the flour (150 g [1¼ cups]), the schmaltz, water, yeast, and salt. Place the bowl back on the mixer and fit it with the dough hook. On low speed, mix the ingredients together until combined, then add the remaining 150 g [1¼ cups] of flour. Mix until there are no dry patches of flour remaining.

2 Stop to scrape down the sides of the bowl, then cover the bowl with a clean tea towel and let the dough rest for 10 minutes to allow the flour to hydrate evenly.

3 Uncover the bowl, turn the mixer speed to medium, and let it run for 5 full minutes, until thoroughly combined. Lightly flour a work surface and, using a flexible scraper, transfer the dough from the bowl to the floured surface. Fold the dough over on itself, rotate a quarter turn, and fold the dough over again. **CONT'D**

4 Fold, turn, and fold four more times. The dough will be wet. Transfer the dough to a lightly greased bowl, cover, and let it rise at room temperature for 1 hour. (Alternatively, coat a zip-top plastic bag lightly with cooking spray and place the dough inside. Do not seal the bag, so the dough has room to rise. Keep the dough in the refrigerator for up to 2 days. Bring to room temperature before proceeding.)

5 To make the topping, in a Dutch oven over medium-high heat, warm the schmaltz until it shimmers. Add the onions and salt, stir to coat with the schmaltz, then lower the heat to medium-low. Cook, stirring regularly, for about 25 minutes, until the onions are soft, entirely wilted, and slightly tan. Transfer them to a bowl and stir in the bread crumbs. Cover and set aside.

6 Preheat the oven to 450°F [230°C]. Line a baking sheet with parchment paper and brush with schmaltz. Scrape the dough onto the parchment-lined baking sheet and press it out into a 10 by 14 in [25 by 35.5 cm] rectangle. If the dough fights with you and bounces back, let it rest for 10 minutes and start again. Once it's pressed out evenly, dimple the top of the dough. Brush the surface with schmaltz and scatter the cooked onion mixture all across the surface. Drizzle again with a little schmaltz, sprinkle with the finishing salt, and slide the parchment paper with the pletzel into the oven. Bake until golden brown, 20 to 25 minutes. Check the internal temperature to be certain; it should register 190°F [88°C].

7 To serve, slice down the center and then into twelve soldiers or rectangles, each about 2 by 5 in [5 by 12 cm].

8 Wrap the rectangles tightly as soon as they're cool and eat within 1 day. Pletzels do not freeze well.

SCHMALTZ

IF YOU WERE RAISED in a gastronomically Ashkenazi Jewish home, you are surely familiar with this Yiddish term for rendered chicken fat. In fact, schmaltz can be made with duck or goose fat, as well as the more common chicken fat. European Jews have a long history of turning to these birds as sources of their cooking fats.

IT IS POSSIBLE TO PURCHASE rendered schmaltz in some grocery stores and kosher markets, but I make my own if only for the heavenly by-product, oh-so-naughty gribenes, the crispy bits of onion and chicken skin that remain after rendering. My grandmother Mary taught me about gribenes and would spoon some on a thin piece of challah, add a pinch of salt, and together we would share this crunchy, salty snack while preparing Sabbath dinner.

MAKE IT A HABIT to save and freeze the fat from chickens as you clean them and prepare them for cooking. Include the soft yellow fat under the breast skin and the tail end called the pope's nose. I keep a small container in the freezer, and when I have enough bits of fat—at least 95 g [½ cup]—I defrost, chop, and render it.

TO RENDER SCHMALTZ AT HOME, chop the fat into small pieces, about the size of an almond, including any skin. If it is slightly frozen or very cold, it's easier to cut up. Place the chopped fat and 56 g [¼ cup] of water in a small saucepan over medium-low heat. Once a slick of melted fat appears on the bottom of the pan, add 1 or 2 Tbsp of finely minced onion. Stir from time to time. Once the mixture is half melted, increase the heat to medium and simmer the fat until it is golden and clear and the browned bits are floating on the top. Strain the schmaltz through a fine-mesh sieve into a clean jar and cover. Enjoy the solids—the gribenes—right away as my grandmother and I did. Refrigerate the schmaltz and use within 1 month. Schmaltz may be frozen for up to 6 months.

THE BIALY

MAKES 6

For the topping

- 2 TBSP OLIVE OIL
- 500 G [4 CUPS] THINLY SLICED YELLOW ONIONS (ABOUT 2 MEDIUM ONIONS SLICED INTO HALF-MOONS)
- ½ TSP KOSHER SALT
- 2 TBSP PLAIN DRIED BREAD CRUMBS
- 2 TO 3 TSP POPPY SEEDS

For the bialys

- 330 G [2¾ CUPS] HIGH-GLUTEN FLOUR, PLUS MORE FOR DUSTING (SEE FLOUR, PAGE 19, FOR SUBSTITUTIONS)
- 168 G [¾ CUP] WATER
- 1½ TSP KOSHER SALT
- ½ TSP INSTANT YEAST
- 3 TBSP CORNMEAL, FOR DUSTING

BIALYSTOKER KUCHEN are rarely sighted these days, but there was a time when bialys were ubiquitous in bagel shops. Crackly and chewy, bialys are never sweet and most often are sprinkled or filled with onions. I've seen bialys topped with onions and potato, with onions and cheese, and with onions dashed with poppy seeds, which was my favorite and serves as the inspiration for this recipe. Some people are ambivalent about poppy seeds; omit them if you fall into that camp.

Cook the onions until wilted and just slightly golden but not deeply caramelized, or they will lose structure and can turn bitter while the bialy is baking. I prefer my onions cut into half-moons, making long, silky strings, but some prefer them diced small so that they turn almost jammy. It's a personal decision.

The biggest challenge to making bialys is coping with over-proofing. Bialys want to dome up and become a dinner roll. Be very attentive during the dough's two rises, particularly the second one, which (in a warm kitchen) can complete in 15 minutes. If they dome in the oven, I promise they'll still taste good.

1 To make the topping, in a Dutch oven or wide, heavy skillet over medium-high heat, warm the oil until it shimmers. Add the onions and salt, stir to coat with the oil, then lower the heat to medium-low. Cook, stirring regularly, for about 25 minutes, until the onions are soft, entirely wilted, and only slightly tan. **CONT'D**

2 Transfer them to a bowl and stir in the bread crumbs and poppy seeds. Cover and set aside to cool.

3 To make the bialys, place the bowl of a stand mixer on a kitchen scale and tare the weight to zero. Measure in the flour, water, salt, and yeast. Place the bowl back on the mixer and fit it with the dough hook. On low speed, mix the ingredients together until there are no dry patches of flour showing (see Mixing, page 32).

4 Stop to scrape down the sides of the bowl and increase the speed to medium. Mix until the sides of the bowl are nearly clean, 2 to 3 minutes. Cover the bowl with a clean tea towel and let the dough rest for 10 minutes to allow the flour to hydrate evenly.

5 Uncover the bowl, turn the mixer speed back to medium, and let it run for 5 full minutes, until the dough is smooth and satiny and the sides of the bowl are clean. The dough will be slightly sticky. Cover the bowl tightly with plastic wrap and let the dough rise for 45 minutes to 1 hour, until doubled in size.

6 Place a pizza stone, Baking Steel, or inverted baking sheet on the center rack of the oven and preheat the oven to 450°F [230°C] for at least 30 minutes.

7 Place a 9 by 13 in [23 by 33 cm] piece of parchment on a pizza peel, large cutting board, or an inverted baking sheet. (You need to be able to easily slide the bialy-laden parchment paper from this surface into the oven.) Dust with the cornmeal.

8 Generously flour a work surface and scrape the dough out of the bowl onto the floury surface. Turn the dough over to coat with flour while deflating, pressing it out into a rectangle. Divide the dough into six equal pieces, each weighing about 85 g [3 oz]. Return to the first portion you weighed and flatten it into a disk, then lift and pull the edges in toward the center to form a ball. Place it seam-side down, and roll the ball under your cupped palm to form a snug, smooth exterior. Repeat with the remaining portions, working in the same order in which they were weighed, to form a total of six balls.

9 Working sequentially, starting with the first ball, flatten it into a disk 5 in [12 cm] across. Lift the disk and, holding it by the edge, turn it to form an outer rim, as though working in a pizzeria window, then place it on the parchment paper and use your fingertips to flatten the center. Work diligently to press out any air bubbles, and use your fingertips to dimple the surface in the center of the dough disk, pressing down with vigor, right through the dough until you feel the work surface.

The bialys should be flat in the center with a rim. Repeat with the remaining dough balls. By the time you finish, you may notice that the first bialy has shrunk down to about 3½ to 4 in [9 to 10 cm] across. That's okay.

10 Cover the baking sheet with a clean tea towel and proof for 15 to 30 minutes at room temperature, until puffy and a fingerprint remains in the dough when it's pressed.

11 Repeat the dimpling process, pressing out a 2 to 3 in [5 to 7.5 cm] area for the topping and leaving a chubby edge. Place about 10 g [a scant ¼ cup] of the onion topping in the center of each disk and spread it until it touches the chubby rim.

12 Slide the parchment paper with the bialys directly onto the hot surface in the oven and bake until pale tan, 13 to 16 minutes. Transfer on their paper to a wire rack to cool for 5 minutes, then cover with a clean tea towel so they steam a bit and stay soft.

13 Bialys will turn stale quickly, so stash them in a bag or covered storage container as soon as they are cool and eat within 1 day, at most. Better yet, share with another bialy fan because they're a rare treat. Bialys do not freeze well.

WHERE IN THE WORLD IS BIALYSTOK?

In her 2000 book, *The Bialy Eaters: The Story of a Bread and a Lost World*, the veteran food writer Mimi Sheraton records her journey to find the birthplace of the bialy. It's a remarkable read, full of detail and rich history. The story of the Bialystocker Jews, like so many communities in the corner of what is now northeastern Poland, is harsh and unforgiving. They suffered inconceivable losses, between the Russian pogroms in the late nineteenth and early twentieth century, Hitler's Germany, and Stalin's Russia. In spite of that, their reputation persists as the greatest bakers of the bialy—and its most enthusiastic eaters. Sheraton recounts locating the last of the Bialystok Jews, all Holocaust survivors. They wistfully recall this daily bread, the rough-and-ready oniony roll we know as a bialy.

THE GLUTEN-FREE BAGEL

MAKES 8

For the bagels

- 445 G [3⅔ CUPS] GLUTEN-FREE ALL-PURPOSE FLOUR, PLUS MORE FOR DUSTING
- 314 G [1⅓ CUPS] WARM WATER, 100°F [35°C]
- 115 G [SCANT 1 CUP] MODIFIED TAPIOCA STARCH (EXPANDEX)
- 70 G [⅔ CUP] UNFLAVORED WHEY PROTEIN POWDER/ISOLATE
- 42 G [2 TBSP] WILDFLOWER HONEY OR OTHER LIGHT-COLORED HONEY
- 2½ TSP KOSHER SALT
- 1½ TSP INSTANT YEAST

For the water bath

- 3 QT [2.8 L] WATER
- 1 TBSP PLUS 1½ TSP HONEY
- 1 TBSP BAKING SODA
- 1 TSP KOSHER SALT

For the egg wash and toppings

- 1 EGG BEATEN WITH ⅛ TSP KOSHER SALT
- TOPPINGS, OPTIONAL (SEE PAGE 48)

SOME GREAT THINGS HAVE BEEN HAPPENING with gluten-free options for traditional bakery items, yet friends with celiac disease complain vociferously about GF bagels. I have little experience with gluten-free baking, but I happen to know a pastry chef who does: Alexandra Mudry of DC's Buttercream Bakeshop worked with me to make this recipe tasty and accessible. These GF bagels have a particularly remarkable chew and crust.

For the most dependable results, use King Arthur Gluten-Free Measure-for-Measure Flour for its high ratio of rice flours that provide starch and benefit the crust. The other major brand, Cup-4-Cup, will produce a slightly softer bagel. Use instant, not active dry or RapidRise, yeast. Two other ingredients (available online and in stores) contribute to the structure and cannot be substituted: To emulate the high protein content of high-gluten flour, you'll need whey protein powder (just like the weightlifters use, and make sure it's unflavored) and modified tapioca starch, often labeled Expandex, which can only be found online (not the tapioca flour in the grocery store). You'll get the best results when these ingredients are measured by weight, not volume. **CONT'D**

1 To make the bagels, place the bowl of a stand mixer on a kitchen scale and tare the weight to zero. Measure in the gluten-free flour, water, modified tapioca starch, whey protein powder, honey, salt, and yeast. Place the bowl back on the mixer and fit it with the dough hook. On medium-low speed, mix the ingredients together for 3 to 4 minutes, until the dough just comes together.

2 Stop to scrape down the bowl once or twice, bringing any dry ingredients up from the bottom, and increase the speed to medium-high. Mix for 5 minutes, stopping to scrape down the dough from the sides midway through; it will be cohesive, puffy, and tender.

3 Use cooking spray to coat a bowl or container large enough to accommodate the dough once doubled in size. Gently transfer the dough to the bowl, being careful not to deflate the dough. Cover the bowl tightly with plastic wrap that has been lightly coated with cooking spray and refrigerate for at least 12 hours and no more than 24 hours.

4 Dust a work surface with flour. Gently scrape the rested dough onto the floured surface and very gently work the dough for a full 3 minutes using a soft fold-and-turn motion rather than actively deflating the dough with vigorous kneading. Under-kneading will result in a disappointing bagel.

5 Line a baking sheet with a 9 by 13 in [23 by 33 cm] piece of parchment paper dusted with flour. Divide the dough into eight equal pieces, each weighing 120 g [about 4¼ oz]. Lightly dust the work surface with more flour, as needed. Return to the first portion you weighed and flatten it into a disk, then lift and pull in the edges toward the center to form a ball. Place it seam-side down and roll the ball under your cupped palm to form a snug, smooth exterior. Repeat with the remaining portions, working in the same order in which they were weighed. Place the balls of dough on the parchment-lined baking sheet, spaced about 2 in [5 cm] apart.

6 Fill a medium bowl with cool water. Dip your fingers into the water and use it to smooth the exterior of each dough ball. With your two dampened index fingers, poke a hole in the center of a dough ball, stretching the hole until it is about 1 in [2.5 cm] across. Dip your fingers again and smooth the surface of the formed bagel. Cover the bagels with plastic wrap that has been lightly coated with cooking spray and let rest at room temperature until doubled in size, about 1 hour.

7 In the meantime, place a pizza stone, Baking Steel, or inverted baking sheet on the oven's center rack and preheat the oven to 400°F [200°C].

8 To make the water bath when ready to boil and bake, in a 5 qt [4.7 L] or larger pot over high heat, combine the water, honey, baking soda, and salt and bring to a boil, then lower the heat to maintain a simmer. Place a 9 by 13 in [23 by 33 cm] piece of parchment paper on a pizza peel, large cutting board, or an inverted baking sheet. (You need to be able to easily slide the bagel-laden parchment paper from this surface into the oven.)

9 Using two hands, gently lift one bagel at a time and carefully lower it into the simmering water. Repeat with another one or two bagels only if they fit in the pot without crowding. It's likely they will sink before rising to the surface. Simmer for 1 minute, then gently turn the bagel over using a slotted spoon or spider. Simmer for another 45 seconds to 1 minute, then gently lift the bagel and place it on the parchment paper. Repeat with the remaining bagels. Brush the bagels gently with the egg wash and sprinkle with toppings, as desired. Slide the parchment paper with the bagels directly onto the hot surface in the oven and bake until deeply golden brown, 16 to 18 minutes. To remove the bagels from the oven, slide the parchment paper right onto the peel. Transfer on their paper to a wire rack to cool.

10 Freshly baked gluten-free bagels need plenty of time to cool so the crumb sets properly. Allow them to rest for 30 to 45 minutes before eating. These bagels are best served the day they are made. Eat within 4 hours or store (see Storing, page 40).

THE GRANOLA BAGEL

MAKES 6

3 TBSP CORNMEAL, FOR DUSTING

420 G [3½ CUPS] HIGH-GLUTEN FLOUR (SEE FLOUR, PAGE 19, FOR SUBSTITUTIONS)

225 G [1 CUP] WATER

21 G [1 TBSP] MAPLE SYRUP

1½ TSP KOSHER SALT

1 TSP INSTANT YEAST

100 G [1 CUP] OLIVE OIL MAPLE GRANOLA (PAGE 77)

MY HUSBAND loves the granola I make, so I created this bagel just for him. He thinks it's just right with a swipe of crunchy peanut butter and a swath of raspberry jam.

Any granola will work here, but I prefer one without dried fruit since dried fruit needs to be plumped before baking, as in the Cinnamon Raisin Bagel (page 57). The granola adds heft to the dough, but it can also dry it out. Make sure to break up any clumps of granola before adding it to the dough, and knead the dough for the full 7 minutes, even if it looks ready sooner.

1 Line a baking sheet with parchment paper and scatter the cornmeal evenly across the paper. Set aside.

2 Place the bowl of a stand mixer on a kitchen scale and tare the weight to zero. Measure in the flour, water, maple syrup, salt, and yeast. Place the bowl back on the mixer and fit it with the dough hook. On low speed, mix the ingredients together until there are no dry patches of flour showing (see Mixing, page 32).

3 Stop to scrape down the sides of the bowl and increase the speed to medium. Mix until the sides of the bowl are nearly clean, 2 to 3 minutes. The dough may seem dry. Cover the bowl with a clean tea towel and let the dough rest for 20 minutes to allow the flour to hydrate evenly.

4 Uncover the bowl, add the granola, turn the mixer speed back to medium, and let it run for 7 full minutes, until the dough is smooth and satiny and the sides of the bowl are clean. Watch the mixer at all times, as it might hop across the counter; the dough will be stiff and strong. **CONT'D**

5 Scrape the dough onto a clean, unfloured work surface and give it five or six kneads. Divide the dough into six equal pieces, each weighing about 130 g [4½ oz]. Shape the bagels (see Shaping, page 33) and place them on the prepared baking sheet. Cover the baking sheet tightly with plastic wrap that has been lightly coated with cooking spray and refrigerate overnight, or for at least 8 hours and no more than 14 hours (see Proofing, page 36).

6 When ready to boil and bake, remove the bagels from the refrigerator and uncover, allowing them to come to room temperature while the oven heats and the water boils (see Timing the Bake, page 38). Place a pizza stone, Baking Steel, or inverted baking sheet on the oven's center rack and set the oven to its highest temperature, 450°F to 500°F [230°C to 260°C] in most home appliances (see Baking, page 38). Heat the oven for at least 30 minutes.

7 In the meantime, fill a 5 qt [4.7 L] or larger pot with water and bring it to a hard boil (see Boiling, page 36). Place a 9 by 13 in [23 by 33 cm] piece of parchment on a pizza peel, large cutting board, or an inverted baking sheet. (You need to be able to easily slide the bagel-laden parchment paper from this surface into the oven.)

8 The bagels should be slightly puffed from their overnight rise. Gently lift one at a time, brushing away any excess cornmeal, and drop it into the boiling water. Repeat with another one or two bagels only if they fit in the pot without crowding. Using a slotted spoon or spider, flip the bagels over and over in the water until very slightly puffed and shiny, about 60 seconds and no more than 90 seconds. Small blisters may appear on the surface.

9 Remove the bagels one by one and place cornmeal-side down on the parchment paper on the pizza peel. Repeat with the remaining bagels; six bagels will fit snugly on the parchment paper without touching.

10 Lower the oven temperature to 450°F [230°C]. Slide the parchment paper with bagels directly onto the hot surface in the oven and bake until deeply golden brown and shiny, 12 to 16 minutes (see Baking, page 38). To remove the bagels from the oven, slide the parchment paper right onto the peel. Transfer on their paper to a wire rack to cool.

11 As tempting as it is to grab the hot bagels immediately, allow them to cool entirely before eating. Eat within 4 hours or store (see Storing, page 40).

OLIVE OIL MAPLE GRANOLA

MAKES 8 CUPS [800 G]

267 G [3 CUPS] OLD-FASHIONED ROLLED OATS (NOT QUICK-COOKING)

114 G [1 CUP] RAW SLIVERED ALMONDS

90 G [3/4 CUP] RAW WALNUT HALVES, BROKEN INTO PIECES

86 G [3/4 CUP] RAW PECAN HALVES, BROKEN INTO PIECES

35 G [1/4 CUP] HULLED, UNSALTED RAW SUNFLOWER SEEDS

35 G [1/4 CUP] HULLED, UNSALTED RAW PUMPKIN SEEDS (PEPITAS)

1/4 CUP [60 ML] OLIVE OIL

1/4 CUP [60 ML] MAPLE SYRUP

1 TSP VANILLA EXTRACT

1 TSP GROUND CINNAMON

1/2 TSP KOSHER SALT

FOR GRANOLA BAGEL page 74

I'VE BEEN MAKING THIS GRANOLA for at least half my life. It's easy to stir together, not too sweet, and very flexible. A good rule of thumb is equal parts oats to nuts, and then use whatever mix-ins you have.

1 Preheat the oven to 325°F [165°C]. Line a baking sheet with parchment paper.

2 In a large bowl, stir together the oats, almonds, walnuts, pecans, sunflower seeds, and pumpkin seeds. Add the olive oil, maple syrup, vanilla, cinnamon, and salt. Stir well.

3 Spread the mixture in an even layer across the baking sheet. Bake for 8 minutes, stir, and bake for another 8 minutes.

4 The granola will be slightly browned and crispy with some larger clumps. Transfer the baking sheet to a wire rack to cool completely before packing in an airtight container. The granola will keep for about 2 weeks.

THE BLUEBERRY BAGEL

MAKES 6

- 420 G [3½ CUPS] PLUS 2 TBSP HIGH-GLUTEN FLOUR, PLUS MORE FOR DUSTING (SEE FLOUR, PAGE 19, FOR SUBSTITUTIONS)
- 225 G [1 CUP] WATER
- 21 G [1 TBSP] MILD HONEY
- 1½ TSP KOSHER SALT
- 1 TSP INSTANT YEAST
- ½ TSP GROUND CARDAMOM
- ½ TSP VANILLA EXTRACT
- 105 G [¾ CUP] FROZEN (NOT DEFROSTED) WILD BLUEBERRIES

BLUEBERRY BAGELS ARE PURPLE. Once I wrapped my brain around that fact (because, really, should a bagel be purple?), I accepted the fruity undertone in this chewy bagel. A little cardamom elevates the berry flavor, and honey keeps the bagel sweet without becoming overwhelming. Use the more intensely flavored, small wild blueberries, found frozen at many grocery stores and at Costco, as they retain integrity in their shape rather than dissolving into pulpy blue-green juice.

Use the blueberries directly from the freezer; as the frozen berries defrost, the dough will become increasingly sticky, so this is the only bagel recipe that calls for a flour-dusted work surface. I've devised some workarounds for manipulating the wetter dough, so make sure to read this recipe all the way through before starting so you can work quickly.

1 Line a baking sheet with parchment paper. Set aside.

2 Place the bowl of a stand mixer on a kitchen scale and tare the weight to zero. Measure in 420 g [3½ cups] of the flour and the water, honey, salt, yeast, cardamom, and vanilla. Place the bowl back on the mixer and fit it with the dough hook. On low speed, mix the ingredients together until there are no dry patches of flour showing (see Mixing, page 32).

3 Stop to scrape down the sides of the bowl and increase the speed to medium. Mix until the sides of the bowl are nearly clean, about 2 minutes. The dough may seem dry. Cover the bowl with a clean tea towel and let the dough rest for 20 minutes to allow the flour to hydrate evenly. **CONT'D**

4 Toss the frozen berries with the remaining 2 Tbsp of flour to coat and add them to the bowl. Working quickly, turn the mixer speed back to low and let it work the dough with the berries for 2 to 3 minutes, then stop and scrape the bowl.

5 Alternate running the mixer on medium speed and stopping to fold the dough over the berries by hand until the blueberries are distributed and there are no more pale streaks in the dough, about 2 minutes total. Once the dough forms a ball around the dough hook, let the mixer run on medium speed for 7 full minutes, until the dough is consistently purple, smooth, and satiny and the sides of the bowl are clean. Watch the mixer at all times, as it might hop across the counter; the dough will be stiff and strong.

6 Lightly dust a work surface with flour. Working quickly to keep the blueberries frozen, divide the dough into six equal pieces, each weighing 135 g [about 4¾ oz] each. Dust the work surface with more flour only as needed. Shape the bagels using the Poke 'Em method (see Shaping, page 35) even though they are sticky and difficult. Flour your hands only as needed. Make sure the center hole is large, because the dough will spring back with vigor. As the bagels are shaped, place them on the prepared baking sheet. Cover the baking sheet tightly with plastic wrap that has been lightly coated with cooking spray and refrigerate overnight, or for at least 8 hours and no more than 14 hours (see Proofing, page 36).

7 When ready to boil and bake, remove the bagels from the refrigerator and uncover, allowing them to come to room temperature while the oven heats and the water boils (see Timing the bake, page 38). Place a pizza stone, Baking Steel, or inverted baking sheet on the oven's center rack and turn the oven to its highest temperature, 450°F to 500°F [230°C to 260°C] in most home appliances (see Baking, page 38). Heat the oven for at least 30 minutes.

8 In the meantime, fill a 5 qt [4.7 L] or larger pot with water and bring it to a hard boil (see Boiling, page 36). Place a 9 by 13 in [23 by 33 cm] piece of parchment on a pizza peel, large cutting board, or an inverted baking sheet and grease lightly with cooking spray. (You need be able to easily slide the bagel-laden parchment paper from this surface into the oven.)

9 The bagels will be slightly puffed from their overnight rise and the parchment paper will be very damp. Using scissors, cut the parchment into six squares, one around each bagel. Gently lift one bagel-topped square and drop it into the boiling water. The paper will release; use tongs to remove and discard it. Repeat with another one or two bagels only if they fit in the pot without crowding. Using a slotted spoon or spider, gently flip the bagels over and over in the water until slightly puffed, about 60 seconds and no more than 90 seconds. Small blisters may appear on the surface.

10 Remove the bagels one by one and place right-side up on the parchment paper on the pizza peel. Repeat with the remaining bagels; six bagels will fit snugly on the parchment paper without touching.

11 Lower the oven temperature to 450°F [230°C]. Slide the parchment paper with bagels directly onto the hot surface in the oven and bake until golden brown and freckled, 13 to 18 minutes (see Baking, page 38). To remove the bagels from the oven, slide the parchment paper right onto the peel. Transfer on the paper to a wire rack to cool.

12 As tempting as it is to grab the hot bagels immediately, allow them to cool slightly before eating. Eat within 4 hours or store (see Storing, page 40).

THE HONEY WHEAT AND OAT BAGEL

MAKES 6

- 3 TBSP CORNMEAL, FOR DUSTING
- 300 G [2½ CUPS] HIGH-GLUTEN FLOUR (SEE FLOUR, PAGE 19, FOR SUBSTITUTIONS)
- 80 G [½ CUP PLUS 1 TBSP] WHOLE-WHEAT FLOUR
- 50 G [½ CUP PLUS 1 TBSP] OAT OR SPELT FLOUR
- 225 G [1 CUP] WATER
- 33 G [1 TBSP PLUS 1½ TSP] FULL-FLAVORED HONEY, SUCH AS BUCKWHEAT OR CHESTNUT
- 1½ TSP KOSHER SALT
- 1 TSP INSTANT YEAST
- TOPPINGS, OPTIONAL (SEE PAGE 48)

A WHOLE-GRAIN BAGEL CAN PRESENT CHALLENGES: When only whole-wheat flour is used, the interior can be dense and the crust and color may suffer. A blend of whole-wheat and high-gluten flours maintains the proper texture, but the flavor is dull. Adding oat or spelt flour—both of which impart a distinct, grainy, almost nutty flavor—does the trick. If you don't have oat flour, it's easy to DIY: Simply blitz rolled oats (not quick-cooking or instant oats) in the food processor or high-speed blender until smooth and floury. A few whole oats scattered over the top of the just-boiled bagels makes for a very pretty bagel after baking.

1 Line a baking sheet with parchment paper and scatter the cornmeal evenly across the paper. Set aside.

2 Place the bowl of a stand mixer on a kitchen scale and tare the weight to zero. Measure in the high-gluten, whole-wheat, and oat flours and the water, honey, salt, and yeast. Place the bowl back on the mixer and fit it with the dough hook. On low speed, mix the ingredients together until there are no dry patches of flour showing (see Mixing, page 32).

3 Stop and scrape down the sides of the bowl and increase the speed to medium. Mix until the sides of the bowl are nearly clean, 2 to 3 minutes. The dough may seem dry. Cover the bowl with a clean tea towel and let the dough rest for 20 minutes to allow the flour to hydrate evenly.

4 Uncover the bowl, turn the mixer speed back to medium, and let it run for 7 full minutes, until the dough is smooth and satiny and the sides of the bowl are clean. Watch the mixer at all times, as it might hop across the counter; the dough will be stiff and strong. **CONT'D**

5 Scrape the dough onto a clean, unfloured work surface and give it five or six kneads. Divide the dough into six equal pieces, each weighing 115 g [about 4 oz]. Shape the bagels (see Shaping, page 33) and place them on the prepared baking sheet. Cover the baking sheet tightly with plastic wrap that has been lightly coated with cooking spray and refrigerate overnight, or for at least 8 hours and no more than 14 hours (see Proofing, page 36).

6 When ready to boil and bake, remove the bagels from the refrigerator and uncover, allowing them to come to room temperature while the oven heats and the water boils (see Timing the Bake, page 38). Place a pizza stone, Baking Steel, or inverted baking sheet on the oven's center rack and set the oven to its highest temperature, 450°F to 500°F [230°C to 260°C] in most home appliances (see Baking, page 38). Heat the oven for at least 30 minutes.

7 In the meantime, fill a 5 qt [4.7 L] or larger pot with water and bring it to a hard boil (see Boiling, page 36). Place a 9 by 13 in [23 by 33 cm] piece of parchment on a pizza peel, large cutting board, or an inverted baking sheet. (You need to be able to easily slide the bagel-laden parchment paper from this surface into your oven.)

8 The bagels should be slightly puffed from their overnight rise. Gently lift one at a time, brushing away any excess cornmeal, and drop it into the boiling water. Repeat with another one or two bagels only if they fit in the pot without crowding. Using a slotted spoon or spider, flip the bagels over and over in the water until very slightly puffed and shiny, about 60 seconds and no more than 90 seconds. Small blisters may appear on the surface.

9 Remove the bagels one by one and place cornmeal-side down on the parchment paper on the pizza peel. Sprinkle with any desired toppings while the bagels are still damp. Repeat with the remaining bagels; six bagels will fit snugly on the parchment paper without touching.

10 Lower the oven temperature to 450°F [230°C]. Slide the parchment paper with the bagels directly onto the hot surface in the oven and bake until deeply golden brown and shiny, about 16 minutes (see Baking, page 38). To remove the bagels from the oven, slide the parchment paper right onto the peel. Transfer on their paper to a wire rack to cool.

11 As tempting as it is to grab the hot bagels immediately, allow them to cool slightly before eating. Eat within 4 hours or store (see Storing, page 40).

THE SUN-DRIED TOMATO AND OLIVE BAGEL

MAKES 6

- 3 TBSP CORNMEAL, FOR DUSTING
- 420 G [3½ CUPS] HIGH-GLUTEN FLOUR (SEE FLOUR, PAGE 19, FOR SUBSTITUTIONS)
- 225 G [1 CUP] WATER
- 21 G [1 TBSP] HONEY
- 1½ TSP KOSHER SALT
- 1 TSP INSTANT YEAST
- 56 G [½ CUP] SUN-DRIED TOMATOES IN OLIVE OIL, DRAINED AND CHOPPED SMALL
- 28 G [¼ CUP] PITTED KALAMATA OLIVES, DRAINED, PATTED DRY, AND CHOPPED SMALL
- 25 G [¼ CUP] GRATED PARMIGIANO-REGGIANO, PLUS MORE FOR GARNISH

THE ADDITION OF umami-loaded kalamata olives and sun-dried tomatoes in this recipe results in a sandwich-worthy bagel. I like to slice this bagel, slather with a thick application of fresh ricotta cheese, and slide it under the broiler.

To ensure the olives and tomatoes disperse evenly throughout the dough, chop them into small bits. Sprinkle a little Parm over the bagels before baking to get that deliciously craggy, cheesy top.

1 Line a baking sheet with parchment paper and scatter the cornmeal evenly across the paper. Set aside.

2 Place the bowl of a stand mixer on a kitchen scale and tare the weight to zero. Measure in the flour, water, honey, salt, and yeast. Place the bowl back on the mixer and fit it with the dough hook. On low speed, mix the ingredients together until there are no dry patches of flour showing (see Mixing, page 32).

3 Stop to scrape down the sides of the bowl and increase the speed to medium. Mix until the sides of the bowl are nearly clean, 2 to 3 minutes. The dough may seem dry. Cover the bowl with a clean tea towel and let the dough rest for 20 minutes to allow the flour to hydrate evenly.

4 Toss the tomatoes and olives with the Parmigiano-Reggiano to coat, and add them to the bowl. Use a stiff spatula or spoon to fold the dough over itself several times. Turn the mixer speed back to low and mix until the bits are combined. **CONT'D**

5 Increase the speed to medium and let the mixer run for 7 full minutes, until the dough is smooth and satiny and the sides of the bowl are clean. Watch the mixer at all times, as it might hop across the counter; the dough will be stiff and strong.

6 Scrape the dough onto a clean, unfloured work surface and give it five or six kneads. Divide the dough into six equal pieces, each weighing 135 g [about 4¾ oz]. Shape the bagels (see Shaping, page 33) and place them on the prepared baking sheet. Cover the baking sheet tightly with plastic wrap lightly coated with cooking spray. Refrigerate overnight, or for at least 8 hours and no more than 14 hours (see Proofing, page 36).

7 When ready to boil and bake, remove the bagels from the refrigerator and uncover, allowing them to come to room temperature while the oven heats and the water boils (see Timing the Bake, page 38). Place a pizza stone, Baking Steel, or inverted baking sheet on the oven's center rack and set the oven to its highest temperature, 450°F to 500°F [230°C to 260°C] in most home appliances (see Baking, page 38). Heat the oven for at least 30 minutes.

8 In the meantime, fill a 5 qt [4.7 L] or larger pot with water and bring it to a hard boil (see Boiling, page 36). Place a 9 by 13 in [23 by 33 cm] piece of parchment on a pizza peel, large cutting board, or an inverted baking sheet. (You need to be able to easily slide the bagel-laden parchment paper from this surface into your oven.)

9 The bagels should be slightly puffed from their overnight rise. Gently lift one at a time, brushing away any excess cornmeal, and drop it into the boiling water. Repeat with another one or two bagels only if they fit in the pot without crowding. Using a slotted spoon or spider, flip the bagels over and over in the water until very slightly puffed and shiny, about 60 seconds and no more than 90 seconds. Small blisters may appear on the surface.

10 Remove the bagels one by one and place cornmeal-side down on the parchment paper on the pizza peel. Sprinkle with more Parmigiano-Reggiano while the bagels are still damp. Repeat with the remaining bagels; six bagels will fit snugly on the parchment paper without touching.

11 Lower the oven temperature to 450°F [230°C]. Slide the parchment paper with the bagels directly onto the hot surface in the oven and bake until deeply golden brown and shiny, 12 to 16 minutes (see Baking, page 38). To remove the bagels from the oven, slide the parchment paper right onto the peel. Transfer on their paper to a wire rack to cool.

12 As tempting as it is to grab the hot bagels immediately, allow them to cool slightly before eating. Eat within 4 hours or store (see Storing, page 40).

THE ASIAGO CHEESE AND PEPPERONI BAGEL

MAKES 6

- 3 TBSP CORNMEAL, FOR DUSTING
- 420 G [3½ CUPS] HIGH-GLUTEN FLOUR (SEE FLOUR, PAGE 19, FOR SUBSTITUTIONS)
- 225 G [1 CUP] WATER
- 21 G [1 TBSP] BARLEY MALT SYRUP OR HONEY
- 1½ TSP KOSHER SALT
- 1 TSP INSTANT YEAST
- 140 G [5 OZ] ASIAGO CHEESE, SHREDDED ON THE LARGEST HOLE OF A BOX GRATER
- 56 G [2 OZ] PEPPERONI, GRATED ON THE SMALLER HOLES OF A BOX GRATER OR GROUND FINE IN THE FOOD PROCESSOR (ABOUT 1 CUP)

A CERTAIN NATIONAL BAGEL CHAIN serves an asiago bagel that is very cheesy and makes a superb sandwich. I took a good thing and made it better by adding pepperoni and a snappy, spicy kick. Grind the pepperoni finely; it needs to disperse evenly to avoid oily pockets in the baked bagel. A sprinkling of more cheese on the top of the bagel before baking means a bronzed frico surface. Turkey pepperoni is acceptable but may not be as kicky as pork pepperoni. Omit the pepperoni for vegetarian friends and increase the cheese to 140 g [5 oz] (an additional ½ cup grated).

These bagels dry out quickly. If not consuming within 1 day, freeze them as soon as they are cool.

1 Line a baking sheet with parchment paper and scatter the cornmeal evenly across the paper. Set aside.

2 Place the bowl of a stand mixer on a kitchen scale and tare the weight to zero. Measure in the flour, water, barley malt syrup, salt, and yeast. Place the bowl back on the mixer and fit it with the dough hook. On low speed, mix the ingredients together until there are no dry patches of flour showing (see Mixing, page 32).

3 Stop to scrape down the sides of the bowl and increase the speed to medium. Mix until the sides of the bowl are nearly clean, 2 to 3 minutes. The dough may seem dry. Cover the bowl with a clean tea towel and let the dough rest for 20 minutes to allow the flour to hydrate evenly. CONT'D

4 Add most of the cheese (reserving a small handful for sprinkling on the bagels before baking) and all of the pepperoni to the bowl. Stir in these additions on low speed, stopping to scrape the sides and bottom of the bowl and fold the dough a few times with a stiff spatula until thoroughly combined. Increase the mixer speed to medium and let it run for 7 full minutes, until the dough is smooth and satiny and the sides of the bowl are clean. Watch the mixer at all times, as it might hop across the counter; the dough will be fairly soft.

5 Scrape the dough onto a clean, unfloured work surface and give it five or six kneads. Divide the dough into six equal pieces, each weighing 135 g [about 4¾ oz]. Shape the bagels (see Shaping, page 33) and place them on the prepared baking sheet. Cover the baking sheet tightly with plastic wrap that has been lightly coated with cooking spray and refrigerate overnight, or for at least 8 hours and no more than 14 hours (see Proofing, page 36).

6 When ready to boil and bake, remove the bagels from the refrigerator and uncover, allowing them to come to room temperature while the oven heats and the water boils (see Timing the Bake, page 38). Place a pizza stone, Baking Steel, or inverted baking sheet on the oven's center rack and set the oven to its highest temperature, 450°F to 500°F [230°C to 260°C] in most home appliances (see Baking, page 38). Heat the oven for at least 30 minutes.

7 In the meantime, fill a 5 qt [4.7 L] or larger pot with water and bring it to a hard boil (see Boiling, page 36). Place a 9 by 13 in [23 by 33 cm] piece of parchment on a pizza peel, large cutting board, or an inverted baking sheet. (You need to be able to easily slide the bagel-laden parchment paper from this surface into your oven.)

8 The bagels should be slightly puffed from their overnight rise. Gently lift one at a time, brushing away any excess cornmeal, and drop it into the boiling water. Repeat with another one or two bagels only if they fit in the pot without crowding. Using a slotted spoon or spider, flip the bagels over and over in the water until very slightly puffed and shiny, about 60 seconds and no more than 90 seconds. Small blisters may appear on the surface.

9 Remove the bagels one by one and place cornmeal-side down on the parchment paper on the pizza peel. Sprinkle with the reserved cheese while they are still damp. Repeat with the remaining bagels; six bagels will fit snugly on the parchment paper without touching.

10 Lower the oven temperature to 450°F [180°C]. Slide the parchment paper with the bagels directly onto the hot surface in the oven and bake until golden brown and blistered, 12 to 16 minutes (see Baking, page 38). To remove the bagels from the oven, slide the parchment paper right onto the peel. Transfer on the paper to a wire rack to cool.

11 As tempting as it is to grab the hot bagels immediately, allow them to cool until barely warm before eating. Eat within 4 hours or store (see Storing, page 40).

THE HATCH CHILE JACK BAGEL

MAKES 6

- 3 TBSP CORNMEAL, FOR DUSTING
- 420 G [3½ CUPS] PLUS 2 TBSP HIGH-GLUTEN FLOUR (SEE FLOUR, PAGE 19, FOR SUBSTITUTIONS)
- 225 G [1 CUP] WATER
- 21 G [1 TBSP] HONEY
- 1½ TSP KOSHER SALT
- 1 TSP INSTANT YEAST
- 112 G [4 OZ] MONTEREY JACK OR PEPPER JACK CHEESE, GRATED ON THE LARGE HOLES OF A BOX GRATER (ABOUT ¾ CUP)
- 2 TBSP CANNED DICED GREEN CHILES, DRAINED AND PATTED DRY

THE CHEESE in these bagels makes them both bouncy and light, with a softer crust like that of milk bread. Opt for classic Monterey Jack cheese or add even more chile heat with a pepper Jack. The tender crumb means these bagels will go stale quickly. If not consuming within 1 day, freeze them as soon as they cool.

1 Line a baking sheet with parchment paper and scatter the cornmeal evenly across the paper. Set aside.

2 Place the bowl of a stand mixer on a kitchen scale and tare the weight to zero. Measure in 420 g [3½ cups] of the flour, the water, honey, salt, and yeast. Place the bowl back on the mixer and fit it with the dough hook. On low speed, mix the ingredients together until there are no dry patches of flour showing (see Mixing, page 32).

3 Stop to scrape down the sides of the bowl and increase the speed to medium. Mix until the sides of the bowl are nearly clean, 2 to 3 minutes. The dough may seem dry. Cover the bowl with a clean tea towel and let the dough rest for 20 minutes to allow the flour to hydrate evenly.

4 Toss the cheese and drained chiles with the remaining 2 Tbsp of flour to coat and add them to the dough. Use a stiff spatula to fold the dough over the cheese and chiles several times. Turn the mixer speed back to low and let it mix the dough for about 1 minute, then stop and scrape the bowl and fold the dough two or three times before mixing again. Once the cheese and chiles are evenly distributed, turn the mixer speed to medium and let it run for 7 full minutes, until the dough is smooth and satiny and the sides of the bowl are clean. Watch the mixer at all times, as it might hop across the counter; the dough will be stiff and strong. CONT'D

5 Scrape the dough onto a clean, unfloured work surface and give it five or six kneads. Divide the dough into six equal pieces, each weighing 150 g [about 5¼ oz]. Shape the bagels (see Shaping, page 33) and place them on the prepared baking sheet. Cover the baking sheet tightly with plastic wrap that has been lightly coated with cooking spray and refrigerate overnight, or for at least 8 hours and no more than 14 hours (see Proofing, page 36).

6 When ready to boil and bake, remove the bagels from the refrigerator and uncover, allowing them to come to room temperature while the oven heats and the water boils (see Timing the Bake, page 38). Place a pizza stone, Baking Steel, or inverted baking sheet on the oven's center rack and set the oven to its highest temperature, 450°F to 500°F [230°C to 260°C] in most home appliances (see Baking, page 38). Heat the oven for at least 30 minutes.

7 In the meantime, fill a 5 qt [4.7 L] or larger pot with water and bring it to a hard boil (see Boiling, page 36). Place a 9 by 13 in [23 by 33 cm] piece of parchment on a pizza peel, large cutting board, or an inverted baking sheet. (You need to be able to easily slide the bagel-laden parchment paper from this surface into your oven.)

8 The bagels should be slightly puffed from their overnight rise. Gently lift one at a time, brushing away any excess cornmeal, and drop it into the boiling water. Repeat with another one or two bagels only if they fit in the pot without crowding. Using a slotted spoon or spider, flip the bagels over and over in the water until very slightly puffed and shiny, about 60 seconds and no more than 90 seconds. Small blisters may appear on the surface.

9 Remove the bagels one by one and place cornmeal-side down on the parchment paper on the pizza peel. Repeat with the remaining bagels; six bagels will fit snugly on the parchment paper without touching.

10 Lower the oven temperature to 450°F [180°C]. Slide the parchment paper with bagels directly onto the hot surface in the oven and bake until deeply golden brown and shiny, about 16 minutes (see Baking, page 38). To remove the bagels from the oven, slide the parchment paper right onto the peel. Transfer on the paper to a wire rack to cool.

11 As tempting as it is to grab a hot bagel immediately, allow them to cool slightly before eating. Eat within 4 hours or store (see Storing, page 40).

THE BAGEL DOG

MAKES 6

- 3 TBSP CORNMEAL, FOR DUSTING
- 1 RECIPE NEW YORK BAGEL DOUGH (PAGE 43)
- 6 HEBREW NATIONAL BEEF JUMBO FRANKS (OR SIMILAR)
- 3 TBSP CARAWAY SEEDS, OPTIONAL

WHO WAS THE FIRST bagel baker to wrap dough around a smoky kosher hot dog? I want to give that baker a hug. Don't give this treatment the side eye: Your friends and family will giggle with glee and dig right in. Dipping sauces and condiments like honey mustard, hot pickle relish, Kewpie mayo, and ranch dressing are part of the fun.

1 Line a baking sheet with parchment paper and scatter the cornmeal evenly across the paper. Set aside.

2 Follow the recipe for the bagel dough through the 7-minute mixer knead, then scrape the dough onto an unfloured work surface. Divide the dough into six equal pieces, each weighing 110 g [just under 3⅞ oz].

3 Shape each portion into a rope about 10 in [25 cm] long. Coil one rope around a hot dog, pinching the tail end firmly to the coiled dough. (This is the trickiest part: Make sure to pinch hard so it doesn't come undone in the boiling water bath.) The ends of the hot dog will be exposed. Place seam-side down on the prepared baking sheet and repeat with the remaining hot dogs and dough portions. Cover the baking sheet tightly with plastic wrap that has been lightly coated with cooking spray and refrigerate over-night, or for at least 8 hours and no more than 14 hours (see Proofing, page 36).

4 When ready to boil and bake, remove the bagels from the refrigerator and uncover, allowing them to come to room temperature while the oven heats and the water boils (see Timing the Bake, page 38). Place a pizza stone, Baking Steel, or inverted baking sheet on the oven's center rack and set the oven to its highest temperature, 450°F to 500°F [230°C to 260°C] in most home appliances (see Baking, page 38). Heat the oven for at least 30 minutes.

5 In the meantime, fill a 5 qt [4.7 L] or larger pot with water and bring it to a hard boil (see Boiling, page 36). Place a 9 by 13 in [23 by 33 cm] piece of parchment on a pizza peel, large cutting board, or an inverted baking sheet. (You need to be able to easily slide the bagel-laden parchment paper from this surface into your oven.) **CONT'D**

6 The bagel dough wrapped around the hot dogs will be slightly puffed from their overnight rise. Gently lift one at a time, using a slotted spoon or spider, and drop it into the boiling water. Repeat with another one or two bagel dogs only if they fit in the pot without crowding. Use the slotted spoon or spider to flip the dogs over and over in the water until the dough is very slightly puffed and shiny, about 60 seconds and no more than 90 seconds. Small blisters may appear on the surface of the dough.

7 Remove the bagel dogs one by one and place cornmeal-side down on the parchment paper on the pizza peel. Sprinkle with the caraway seeds, if using, while the bagel dogs are still damp. Repeat with the remaining bagel dogs; six will fit snugly on the parchment paper without touching.

8 Lower the oven temperature to 425°F [220°C]. Slide the parchment paper with the bagel dogs directly onto the hot surface in the oven and bake until deeply golden brown and shiny, 16 to 18 minutes (see Baking, page 38). To remove the bagel dogs from the oven, slide the parchment paper right onto the peel. Transfer on their paper to a wire rack to cool.

9 As tempting as it is to grab the hot bagel dogs immediately, allow them to cool slightly before eating. Eat within 4 hours or store (see Storing, page 40).

№ 2

FINDING YOUR INNER BALABOOSTA 

— 101 —

SAVORY 107

SCHMEARS

IF YOU EAT ALL YOUR BAGELS, YOU'LL HAVE NOTHING IN YOUR POCKET BUT THE HOLES. —YIDDISH PROVERB

CHERRY
CHEESECAKE CHEESE
page 127
DRIED APRICOT, COCONUT,
AND THYME CHEESE
page 130
PIMENTO CHEDDAR
CHEESE
page 116

LOX CHEESE
page 111

VEGGIE CHEESE
page 115

CANNOLI CHEESE
page 129

FINDING YOUR INNER BALABOOSTA

OF ALL THE YIDDISH WORDS I grew up hearing, *balaboosta* was the one that my great-grandmother, Agatha Rosenheim Solomon, wore like a pageant sash. Known as Nonna to family and friends, she was an impressively competent homemaker—a balaboosta. She was my grandfather Ben's mother, a late-1800s immigrant from Germany in an area of what is now Poland. A bootstrapper, she was abandoned by her husband Meyer (although she preferred to tell a more colorful story) and raised her two sons alone, crossing the country from Chicago to California to Michigan, working as a corset saleswoman. By the time I was born, she had been on her own for more than forty years.

Between the ages of five and eleven, I spent a good part of each summer at Nonna's house. At this time, she was already in her seventies and was determined to do everything herself. Her son and grandson worried, and that's why I became her "assistant"—to keep her from climbing ladders or spending too many hours in the hot kitchen. I spent those summers picking strawberries from the garden and making jam, sewing aprons for the Temple gift shop, baking hundreds of rugelach for bake sales, or rubbing beeswax into the heavy, carved furniture.

Agatha had another reason to encourage my visits: In her eyes, my mother was a modern woman. Agatha worried about my balaboosta education and made no bones about it. She would pick up knitting needles and yarn and say, "Your mother will never teach you how to do this, so I will." While working in the garden, "I'm guessing your mother doesn't know when to pull the onions." While packing cucumbers into jars, "The Solomon women make their own pickles." You get the picture.

I'm grateful to have had those times with Nonna and for the skills that endure. It was Agatha who taught me to whip sour cream into store-bought cream cheese to make it more spreadable, to pluck chives from the garden and cut them into tiny pieces with kitchen shears, to soak onions in cold water to cut the bite. Balaboosta recipes are dotted through the next pages—DIY cream cheese, sour cream, and pickles—all evidence that I'm doing my best to join the ranks of the balaboosta.

BALABOOSTA CREAM CHEESE

MAKES ABOUT 12 OZ [340 G]

2 CUPS [475 ML] WHOLE MILK

2 CUPS [475 ML] HEAVY CREAM (NOT ULTRA-PASTEURIZED)

½ CUP [120 ML] FULL-FAT BUTTERMILK

¼ TSP KOSHER OR FINE SEA SALT

HOMEMADE CREAM CHEESE is silky and creamy—much softer than the blocks in the grocery store—a schmear in and of itself. It's just the right consistency for the add-ins (see pages 107 to 133) too. Use the very best dairy you can find: organic, certainly, and from a local farm is ideal. Cream-top milk makes beautiful cream cheese. You'll need a threadbare cotton or linen towel or a double layer of fine cheesecloth and some twine, as well as a place to hang the cheese as it drains. Allow 4 days for culturing and draining.

1 In a 3 qt [2.8 L] or larger saucepan over low heat, bring the milk and cream to 75°F [24°C]. Remove from the heat and gently stir in the buttermilk.

2 Cover and wrap the pan in a clean tea towel and place it in a warm, draft-free spot to culture the mixture. (If your kitchen counter is made of stone, marble, or some other cool-to-the-touch material, place it somewhere else.) In about 24 hours, a small amount of whey should separate from the curd, which will become thick like Greek yogurt. If there seems to be mostly liquid under thick cream, the culturing has not finished. This step can take as long as 36 hours. The firmer the curd, the easier the next steps will be. **CONT'D**

3 Once the culturing has finished and you have a thick curd, line a colander with the tea towel and place the colander over a large bowl. Transfer with a spider or slowly pour the cultured cheese into the colander and let it drain for 30 minutes. There should be about 1 cup [235 ml] of whey. Reserve for another use or discard.

4 Gather the towel by all four corners, turning one corner around to knot the towel into a pouch. Bind a length of kitchen twine around the knot. With the twine, tie the pouch securely to a cabinet handle, faucet handle, or any place it can be suspended over a bowl. This setup uses gravity to drain the rest of the whey from the cheese. Place a bowl under the pouch and let it drain for 8 hours. The ideal temperature for the space is 78°F [26°C]—if it's cooler, it may take longer for the cheese to form. If it's warmer than 85°F [29°C], the cheese will spoil.

5 After 8 hours, place a large piece of plastic wrap or wax paper on a cutting board. Untie the pouch and scrape the cheese onto the covered board. The cheese should be smooth and thick and hold together; it will firm up further in the refrigerator. If it is still liquidy in the center, return it to the towel, retie the pouch, and hang it for another 2 to 6 hours.

6 Add the salt to the cheese and use a flexible bench scraper to incorporate it. Salt helps extend the cream cheese's life. It will dissolve through the cream cheese, so only a couple of folds will do the trick. Use the plastic wrap or wax paper to form the cheese into a log or a block. Chill for at least 8 hours.

7 The cream cheese will keep for up to 2 weeks in the refrigerator.

SCHMEAR MASTER RECIPE

MAKES 9 OZ [255 G]

- 8 OZ [225 G] FULL-FAT CREAM CHEESE, SOFTENED
- 2 TBSP SOUR CREAM OR CRÈME FRAÎCHE
- ½ TSP FRESH LEMON JUICE

AT THE BREAKFAST TABLE, it's perfectly acceptable to serve up a rectangular brick of Philadelphia cream cheese in its original form. It has the same familiarity as a cylinder of canned cranberry sauce on the Thanksgiving table. A bagel brunch, though, deserves a schmear, which is different from that block of cream cheese. It is more spreadable and creamy, and is the vehicle for flavorful additions.

Start with this recipe. Consider it the foundational schmear, and put variety on the brunch table using the add-in recipes that follow (see pages 107 to 133).

A tasty schmear starts with good cream cheese. When you have the time and inclination, try the Balaboosta Cream Cheese (page 103), because it is so very tangy and smooth. If I'm not making my own from scratch, Philadelphia is my go-to brand. If you can find it, the fluffy Temp Tee whipped cream cheese (look in kosher markets) is an old-school favorite. For the truest, milkiest flavor, avoid stabilizer-laced or low-fat versions of cream cheese.

1 In the bowl of a stand mixer fitted with the paddle attachment, combine the cream cheese, sour cream, and lemon juice, increasing the speed as the ingredients combine, until fluffy, lightened, and spreadable, just 1 to 2 minutes. Alternatively, use a medium mixing bowl and a stiff spoon to combine and then stir and whip vigorously to aerate and lighten the mixture.

2 Pack the schmear into a ramekin or two, cover, and chill until ready to serve. It will keep for 1 week in the refrigerator.

NONDAIRY OPTIONS

Shockingly, the majority of the world's population has some lactose intolerance. A 2015 article in *Haaretz* suggested that as many as 75 percent of Jews across the world could be lactose intolerant. Every recipe in this chapter may be made with vegan cream cheese, vegan butter, and vegan sour cream, substituting for the corresponding dairy-laden ingredients. And while schmears are part of every classic bagel brunch, remember to include some alternatives: Hummus and peanut or almond butter, cheeses made from cashews or other nuts, honey, and fruit jams are easy options for dairy-avoiders.

CHIVE CHEESE
page 107

BACON SCALLION CHEESE
page 109

SCALLION CHEESE
page 108

CHIVE CHEESE

MAKES 10 OZ [280 G]

- 1 SCHMEAR MASTER RECIPE (PAGE 105)
- ¼ CUP [15 G] FINELY CHOPPED FRESH CHIVES
- ½ TSP FRESH LEMON JUICE
- ¼ TSP FRESHLY GROUND BLACK PEPPER

CHIVES ARE MAGNIFICENT in early spring, especially when freshly cut from a garden just coming to life. I have had a lifelong love affair with chives, and this is my favorite schmear of all, particularly when it's in season. Snip chives with sharp kitchen shears for the tiny pieces that make this schmear so pretty. If you make this cheese when the edible chive flowers are blooming, fold a few purple flower petals into the schmear and decorate the surface with two or three whole flowers. It must be my Russian genes—I love chive cheese on an onion bagel.

1 In a medium bowl, add the schmear, chives, lemon juice, and pepper. Stir with a fork until thoroughly combined.

2 Pack the schmear into a ramekin or two, cover, and chill until ready to serve. It will keep for about 2 days in the refrigerator before its oniony flavor becomes overwhelming.

SCALLION CHEESE

MAKES 10 OZ [280 G]

- ⅓ CUP [20 G] FINELY CHOPPED SCALLIONS, WHITE AND LIGHT GREEN PARTS ONLY
- 1 SCHMEAR MASTER RECIPE (PAGE 105)
- ¼ TSP KOSHER SALT

WHEN CHIVES ARE NO LONGER IN SEASON, I turn to scallion cream cheese for a similarly zingy onion flavor. But scallions carry a little too much oomph for me, so I soak them in cold water for a few minutes to mellow some of the bite. Make sure to dry the scallions on a cloth towel before adding to the schmear. (Never terrycloth, and not paper towels. The scallion bits stick. Very annoying.)

1 In a small bowl, cover the chopped scallions with cold water for 10 minutes. Drain and dry the scallions on a cloth towel.

2 In a medium bowl, add the schmear, scallions, and salt. Stir with a fork until thoroughly combined.

3 Pack the scallion cheese into a ramekin or two, cover, and chill until ready to serve. It will keep for about 2 days in the refrigerator before the oniony flavor becomes overwhelming.

BACON SCALLION CHEESE

MAKES 10 OZ [280 G]

1/3 CUP [20 G] FINELY CHOPPED SCALLIONS, WHITE AND LIGHT GREEN PARTS ONLY

1 SCHMEAR MASTER RECIPE (PAGE 105)

1/3 CUP [115 G] CRISPED AND MINCED SMOKED BACON (ABOUT 4 SLICES)

1/4 TO 1/2 TSP FRESHLY GROUND BLACK PEPPER

ON THE WAY TO Woods Hole, Massachusetts, where the ferries run to Martha's Vineyard and Nantucket, Cape Cod Bagel makes a very good bagel. The scallion and bacon cream cheese I had there was magnificent, and this is my attempt to replicate it. Chop the bacon and scallions into very small pieces to make this schmear especially spreadable. Soaking the chopped scallions in cold water mellows their oniony bite. When spread on an egg bagel, this is a new twist on the bacon, egg, and cheese sandwich.

1 In a small bowl, cover the chopped scallions with cold water for 10 minutes. Drain and dry the scallions on a cloth towel.

2 In a medium bowl, add the schmear, bacon, scallions, and pepper. Stir with a fork until thoroughly combined.

3 Pack the bacon scallion cheese into a ramekin or two, cover, and chill until ready to serve. It will keep for about 2 days in the refrigerator before its oniony flavor becomes overwhelming.

HOT-SMOKED
SALMON CHEESE
page 112
LOX CHEESE
page 111

LOX CHEESE

MAKES 12 OZ [340 G]

- 1 SCHMEAR MASTER RECIPE (PAGE 105)
- ½ CUP [56 G] LOX OR NOVA (COLD SMOKED) SALMON, CHOPPED
- 2 TBSP FINELY CHOPPED FRESH CHIVES
- ½ TSP LEMON ZEST
- 1 TSP FRESH LEMON JUICE
- ¼ TSP FRESHLY GROUND BLACK PEPPER

WHEN THERE'S A LITTLE BIT OF SALMON LEFT OVER—too little for one bagel—chop it into pea-size pieces to make this cheese especially spreadable. I love the bite of fresh chives, but if you don't want the oniony zing, add flat-leaf parsley instead. Spread on sesame bagel chips for a great lunch when served alongside a bowl of soup.

1 In a medium bowl, add the schmear, salmon, chives, lemon zest and juice, and pepper. Stir with a fork until thoroughly combined, with pieces of salmon evenly distributed and still a bit chunky.

2 Pack the lox cheese into a ramekin or two, cover, and chill until ready to serve. It will keep for 1 week in the refrigerator.

HOT-SMOKED SALMON CHEESE

MAKES 12 OZ [340 G]

- 1 SCHMEAR MASTER RECIPE (PAGE 105)
- 1/3 CUP [56 G] FLAKED KIPPERED SALMON
- 2 TBSP FINELY CHOPPED FRESH DILL (OR 2 TSP DRIED DILL)
- 1 TBSP JARRED HORSERADISH
- 1 TSP DRAINED CAPERS, OPTIONAL

KIPPERED, OR HOT-SMOKED, SALMON is flaky and rich. The flavor is intensified and the smoke is distinct. Sometimes called salmon candy, it's easy to make (see page 143) and widely available. This schmear has a significant horseradish kick, so cut back if that's not your thing. While using fresh, raw horseradish may sound like a good idea, it can be woody and hard to chew and has no place in a creamy schmear. Opt for jarred horseradish, found in the refrigerated section of the grocery store.

1 In a medium bowl, add the schmear, salmon, dill, horseradish, and capers, if using. Stir with a fork until thoroughly combined, leaving nuggets of salmon throughout.

2 Pack the hot-smoked salmon cheese into a ramekin or two, cover, and chill until ready to serve. It will keep for about 5 days in the refriger-ator; the horseradish flavor will grow stronger as time passes.

VARIATION

HORSERADISH DILL CHEESE

Omit the salmon and capers from the Hot-Smoked Salmon Cheese recipe. Serve Horseradish Dill Cheese with the Beet-Cured Gravlax (page 149) or Kippered Salmon (page 146).

OLIVE CHEESE

MAKES 10 OZ [280 G]

1 SCHMEAR MASTER RECIPE (PAGE 105)

½ CUP [90 G] FINELY CHOPPED PITTED OLIVES

WHILE I PREFER TO USE GREEN OLIVES (with pimento) in my olive spread, many people prefer black olives. Black olive schmear is easier, because small cans of already-chopped black olives are widely available, but for me, there's no substitute for briny, flavor-forward green olives, dirty martini style. Choose your own olive adventure and schmear your way to a delicious bagel topper: Green, black, chewy kalamata (for more briny tones), or picholine (for their tart tang) all work well in this recipe. Or, go extra fancy by using Spicy Marinated Olives (page 172).

1 In a medium bowl, combine the schmear and olives using a stiff spatula. Stir until thoroughly combined.

2 Pack the olive cheese into a ramekin or two, cover, and chill until ready to serve. It will keep for about 4 days in the refrigerator.

VEGGIE CHEESE

MAKES 10 OZ [280 G]

2 TBSP FINELY DICED RED ONION	1 TBSP CHOPPED FRESH CHIVES
1 SCHMEAR MASTER RECIPE (PAGE 105)	1 TBSP CHOPPED FRESH DILL
2 TBSP FINELY DICED CARROT	1 TBSP CHOPPED FRESH PARSLEY
2 TBSP FINELY DICED CELERY	½ TSP GRATED FRESH GARLIC
1 TBSP FINELY DICED RED BELL PEPPER	¼ TSP FRESHLY GROUND BLACK PEPPER

VEGETABLE-SPIKED CREAM CHEESE is difficult to balance—it requires a thoughtful combination of crunch, seasoning, and herbs in every bite. This recipe gives you a little bit of all three. As with the Scallion Cheese (page 108), soaking the red onion in cold water after chopping mellows its bite.

1 In a small bowl, cover the red onion with cold water. Set aside for 10 minutes. Strain and dry the onions on a cloth towel.

2 In a medium bowl, combine the schmear, red onion, carrot, celery, bell pepper, chives, dill, parsley, garlic, and pepper using a stiff spatula. Stir until thoroughly combined.

3 Pack the veggie cheese into a ramekin or two, cover, and chill until ready to serve. It will keep for 1 week in the refrigerator.

PIMENTO CHEDDAR CHEESE

MAKES 10 OZ [280 G]

- ½ SCHMEAR MASTER RECIPE (PAGE 105)
- 1 CUP [113 G] SHREDDED EXTRA SHARP CHEDDAR CHEESE
- ½ CUP [56 G] SHREDDED SHARP CHEDDAR CHEESE
- 2 TBSP DICED JARRED PIMENTOS, DRAINED
- 1 TBSP MAYONNAISE
- ½ TSP KOSHER SALT
- ¼ TSP FRESHLY GROUND PEPPER
- ⅛ TSP HOT SAUCE, PLUS MORE AS NEEDED

PIMENTO CHEESE wasn't part of my experience growing up, but once I was introduced, it became my new best friend. Those in the eastern and southern United States will insist that the mayonnaise must be Duke's brand (and I agree), but feel free to use the very best mayo available in your area. I like pimento cheese anytime, but especially on a hot summer day with bagel chips (see page 40) and a handful of sun-warmed cherry tomatoes. It's the perfect lunch.

1 In a medium bowl, add the schmear, both Cheddar cheeses, pimentos, mayonnaise, salt, pepper, and hot sauce. Stir with a stiff spatula until thoroughly combined.

2 Pack the pimento cheese into a ramekin or two, cover, and chill until ready to serve. Take it out 30 minutes before serving. It will keep for about 1 week in the refrigerator.

HOT HONEY AND MARCONA ALMOND CHEESE

MAKES 10 OZ [280 G]

1 SCHMEAR MASTER RECIPE (PAGE 105)

1/3 CUP [56 G] SALTED MARCONA ALMONDS, CHOPPED

3 TBSP BALABOOSTA HOT HONEY (RECIPE FOLLOWS) OR STORE-BOUGHT

1/2 TSP SHERRY VINEGAR

A FEW YEARS BACK, a friend included a bottle of hot honey in my holiday gift basket. This chile-spiked condiment soon found its way into, well, everything. In my world, hot honey is a necessary pantry item, and it's easy enough to make at home. This schmear has it all—flavor and texture—in a sweet, hot, salty, crunchy package.

1 In a medium bowl, add the schmear, almonds, hot honey, and vinegar. Stir with a stiff spatula until thoroughly combined.

2 Pack the hot honey and Marcona almond cheese into a ramekin or two, cover, and chill until ready to serve. It will keep for about 1 week in the refrigerator.

BALABOOSTA HOT HONEY

MAKES ½ CUP [170 G]

½ CUP [170 G] LIGHT-COLORED HONEY

1 DRIED CHILE DE ARBOL, STEMMED, SEEDED, AND TORN INTO 2 PIECES, OR 1 FRESH THAI BIRD CHILE, STEMMED, SEEDED, AND HALVED

IT'S CHALLENGING TO REGULATE the heat of homemade hot honey, but I have been very happy with every experiment. Sometimes it seems barely perceptible, a back-of-the-throat burn, and other times I gasp and my eyes water. The longer the chile stays in the honey, the more the flavor will infuse and strengthen. Taste every few hours to see when it's right for you. One of my favorite uses for hot honey is to drizzle it over burrata, fresh cherries or peaches, and toasted hazelnuts.

1 Pour the honey into a ½ pt [240 ml] mason jar (jelly-jar size). Cover lightly with a paper towel and microwave on high in 30-second bursts until the outside of the jar feels warm, about 2 minutes. Add the chile, stir, and microwave for another minute, until the outside of the jar feels hot.

2 Cover the jar and set aside for 24 hours.

3 Remove the chile and reserve for another use, or leave it in and let the Scoville index rise. The honey will keep for 1 month at room temperature.

TRIPLE LEMON CHEESE

MAKES 10 OZ [280 G]

- 1 SCHMEAR MASTER RECIPE (PAGE 105)
- 1/4 CUP [15 G] FLAT-LEAF PARSLEY, FINELY CHOPPED
- 3 TBSP PRESERVED LEMON RIND, DRAINED, RINSED, AND FINELY MINCED
- 1 TBSP LEMON ZEST
- 1 TBSP FRESH LEMON JUICE
- 1/2 TSP KOSHER SALT
- 1/4 TSP FRESHLY GROUND BLACK PEPPER

IF YOU LOVE LEMON, this is your schmear. Preserved lemons are a salty, sour, textural condiment (see the following recipe to make your own). Their sweet tang is an ideal complement to smoked salmon; the combination is multidimensional and adult. My idea of heaven is this schmear on a toasted poppy seed bagel.

1 In a medium bowl, add the schmear, parsley, preserved lemon, lemon zest and juice, salt, and pepper. Stir with a whisk until thoroughly combined. The mixture will want to break, but continuous whisking will smooth it out.

2 Pack the triple lemon cheese into a ramekin or two, cover, and chill until ready to serve. It will keep for about 1 week in the refrigerator.

BALABOOSTA SALT-PRESERVED LEMONS

MAKES 2 CUPS [200 G]

ABOUT 1/3 CUP [48 G] KOSHER SALT

8 ORGANIC LEMONS, RINSED WELL

2 BAY LEAVES

PRESERVED LEMONS lend a salty, tangy zing to many of my regular-rotation dinner recipes. Making them is easy, and once you're hooked, try experimenting with herbs, spices, and chiles. Use the cured lemons by adding the chopped peel to chicken, vegetables, fish, long-cooked stews, and salad dressings. Allow 3 weeks for curing.

1 Wash and dry a lidded 1 pt [480 ml] jar with a wide mouth. Pour in 1 Tbsp of the salt.

2 Slice a lemon lengthwise vertically, as though cutting it into quarters, but stop your knife ½ in [12 mm] from the base so the lemon remains in one piece. Fan out the lemon, opening it up, and rub salt on all the surfaces. Squeeze the lemon back together and push it into the jar. Sprinkle 1 tsp of salt over it. Repeat with three of the remaining lemons.

3 Use a wooden spoon to press down on the lemons in the jar, releasing their juice. Juice the remaining four lemons and add the juice to the jar, submerging the salted lemons. If there is room in the jar, slice, salt, and add the juiced lemons too. Tuck in the bay leaves.

4 Tighten the lid of the jar and leave it at room temperature in a dark place until the lemons are tender, about 3 weeks. Shake the jar daily for the first week, and make sure the lemons remain submerged.

5 Store the preserved lemons for up to 1 month in the refrigerator. To use, scrape away and discard the flesh and use the salty rind, usually minced or cut into narrow strips.

CARROT CAKE CHEESE
page 126
WALNUT RAISIN CHEESE
page 125

WALNUT RAISIN CHEESE

MAKES 10 OZ [280 G]

- ½ CUP [56 G] WALNUTS, TOASTED AND FINELY CHOPPED (SEE NOTE)
- ¼ TSP CARDAMOM SEEDS, FROM ABOUT 6 CARDAMOM PODS, CRUSHED (SEE HEADNOTE)
- 1 SCHMEAR MASTER RECIPE (PAGE 105)
- ¼ CUP [17 G] RAISINS, CHOPPED
- 1 TSP HONEY

WALNUTS ARE RICH, buttery, and sweet and improve when toasted. In this recipe, crush the cardamom seeds while the nuts are toasting. When the warm nuts meet the crushed seeds, the perfume is delightful. Raisins provide a good, chewy, sweet counterpoint; I like to use currants too.

To extract the seeds from cardamom pods, use a meat pounder or the flat bottom of a heavy pot to crack open the pods and release the small black seeds. A mortar and pestle is also useful for crushing the pods to release the seeds and then crushing the seeds. Discard the empty pods. Ground cardamom has about half the aroma of freshly crushed seeds, but if it's all you have, use ½ tsp in this recipe.

1 In a medium bowl, toss together the just-toasted nuts and crushed cardamom seeds. Add the schmear, raisins, and honey and mix together using a stiff spatula until thoroughly combined.

2 Pack the walnut raisin cheese into a ramekin or two, cover, and chill until ready to serve. It will keep for about 5 days in the refrigerator.

HOW TO TOAST NUTS

Nuts become more aromatic and tastier, and their texture improves, with a light toasting. Place them on an unlined baking sheet and toast in a preheated 350°F [180°C] oven for 10 to 12 minutes, until fragrant and lightly browned. Alternatively, place the nuts in a dry, heavy skillet over medium-high heat and toast, keeping them moving so they brown and do not scorch, for 6 to 8 minutes.

CARROT CAKE CHEESE

MAKES 12 OZ [340 G]

- 1 SCHMEAR MASTER RECIPE (PAGE 105)
- ⅓ CUP [30 G] PEELED, SHREDDED CARROT
- ⅓ CUP [70 G] FRESH OR CANNED PINEAPPLE, DRAINED AND FINELY CHOPPED
- ¼ CUP [40 G] ROASTED AND SALTED PISTACHIOS, CHOPPED
- 2 TBSP CANDIED OR CRYSTALLIZED GINGER, CHOPPED
- 2 TBSP CONFECTIONERS' SUGAR
- ½ TSP GROUND CINNAMON

THERE WAS A DELI I frequented in New York City back in the early 1990s where they would schmear carrot cake cream cheese on a sesame bagel. It soon became a favorite afternoon pick-me-up with a cup of coffee. To shred the carrots, use the medium holes on a box grater or a food processor fitted with a grating disk.

1 In a medium bowl, combine the schmear, carrot, pineapple, pistachios, ginger, confectioners' sugar, and cinnamon using a stiff spatula. Stir until thoroughly combined.

2 Pack the carrot cake cheese into a ramekin or two, cover, and chill until ready to serve. It will keep for about 4 days in the refrigerator.

CHERRY CHEESECAKE CHEESE

MAKES 12 OZ [340 G]

1 SCHMEAR MASTER RECIPE (PAGE 105)

½ CUP [60 G] CRUSHED GRAHAM CRACKERS (ABOUT 7 CRACKERS)

¼ CUP [80 G] SOUR CHERRY PRESERVES (SOMETIMES CALLED TART CHERRY)

2 TBSP CONFECTIONERS' SUGAR

½ TSP VANILLA EXTRACT

HERE ARE ALL THE FLAVORS of cheesecake in a schmear. Use preserves with small pieces of fruit, or plan to chop the fruit into smaller pieces before stirring it into the schmear. Graham cracker shards bring to mind the cheesecake crust and add texture. Swap in any preserves on hand. Apricot is delightful, as is plum.

1 In a medium bowl, add the schmear, crushed graham crackers, cherry preserves, sugar, and vanilla. Stir with a fork until thoroughly combined.

2 Pack the cherry cheesecake cheese into a ramekin or two, cover, and chill until ready to serve. It will keep for about 5 days in the refrigerator. The graham crackers will soften over time.

CHERRY CHEESECAKE CHEESE
page 127

CANNOLI CHEESE
page 129

CANNOLI CHEESE

MAKES 10 OZ [280 G]

- 1 SCHMEAR MASTER RECIPE (PAGE 105)
- ½ CUP [90 G] MINI CHOCOLATE CHIPS
- ¼ CUP [56 G] CANDIED ORANGE RIND, CHOPPED
- 3 TBSP MASCARPONE CHEESE
- 3 TBSP CONFECTIONERS' SUGAR
- ½ TSP FRESHLY GRATED ORANGE ZEST

REMINISCENT OF SWEETENED CITRUS-SCENTED cannoli filling, this schmear is delicious on any sweet bagel. It's possible to make the candied orange rind at home, but it's also available at candy shops, at cake supply shops, and online. Candied Meyer lemon is particularly floral, sweet, and tart and a nice swap for the orange rind in this recipe, if you can find it.

1 In a medium bowl, combine the schmear, chocolate chips, candied orange rind, mascarpone, confectioners' sugar, and orange zest using a stiff spatula. Stir until thoroughly combined.

2 Pack the cannoli cheese into a ramekin or two, cover, and chill until ready to serve. It will keep for about 3 days in the refrigerator.

DRIED APRICOT, COCONUT, AND THYME CHEESE

MAKES 9 OZ [255 G]

¼ CUP [23 G] SWEETENED SHREDDED COCONUT

1 SCHMEAR MASTER RECIPE (PAGE 105)

⅓ CUP [65 G] DRIED APRICOTS, CHOPPED

1 TSP FRESH THYME LEAVES

¼ TSP KOSHER SALT

THIS RICH, CHEWY SCHMEAR is sweet and herbal. If the apricots are not plump and soft, soak them in just-boiled water for 5 minutes before chopping into pieces the size of sunflower seeds.

1 In a dry skillet over medium heat, toast the coconut, moving it around the skillet constantly until barely golden brown, 2 to 3 minutes. It will burn quickly; don't turn away.

2 In a medium bowl, add the schmear, toasted coconut, apricots, thyme, and salt. Stir with a fork until thoroughly combined.

3 Pack the dried apricot, coconut, and thyme cheese into a ramekin or two, cover, and chill until ready to serve. It will keep for about 5 days in the refrigerator.

TAMARI ALMOND CANDIED GINGER CHEESE

MAKES 10 OZ [280 G]

1 SCHMEAR MASTER RECIPE (PAGE 105)

¼ CUP [30 G] TAMARI ALMONDS, FINELY CHOPPED (RECIPE FOLLOWS)

2 TBSP CANDIED OR CRYSTALLIZED GINGER, FINELY CHOPPED

1 TSP FRESHLY GRATED LEMON ZEST

½ TSP FRESH LEMON JUICE

FOR THIS TANGY, bright, crunchy, sweet, and chewy schmear, chop the nuts into small but still recognizable pieces for easy spreading. Candied ginger comes in all sizes; chop into pieces the same size as the almonds. Lemon zest rounds out all the flavors.

1 In a medium bowl, combine the schmear, almonds, ginger, lemon zest, and lemon juice with a stiff spatula. Stir until thoroughly combined.

2 Pack the tamari almond candied ginger cheese into a ramekin or two, cover, and chill until ready to serve. It will keep for about 1 week in the refrigerator.

TAMARI ALMONDS

MAKES ABOUT 1½ CUPS [255 G]

8 OZ [225 G] WHOLE RAW ALMONDS

¼ CUP [60 ML] TAMARI (GLUTEN-FREE SOY SAUCE)

THESE ARE A REGULAR SNACK in our house—salty, slightly sweet, and utterly addictive. Pack them for road trips or hikes, or simply grab a handful when the hungries hit.

1 In a medium bowl, stir together the almonds and tamari to coat. Set aside for 20 minutes.

2 Meanwhile, preheat the oven to 325°F [165°C] and line a baking sheet with parchment paper. Tip the almonds and any remaining tamari out onto the baking sheet. Spread out the nuts so they are not touching. Toast for a total of 16 minutes, stirring halfway through. Transfer the pan to a wire rack and stir the nuts. Cool thoroughly before serving or storing in a jar with a tight-fitting lid. The almonds will keep for 1 week at room temperature.

№ 3

A NICE PIECE OF FISH

& OTHER FAVORITES FROM THE APPETIZING STORE

ON TISHA B'AV YOU FAST / AND IT'S NOT RIGHT TO EAT / BEFORE THE FAST YOU HAVE A BAGEL WITH ASH / AND BEFORE YOU FAST YOU HAVE A FULL BOTTLE / UNTIL 3 O'CLOCK YOU RECITE LAMENTS / AFTERWARDS YOU SETTLE YOUR / HUNGRY STOMACH —NINETEENTH-CENTURY LITHUANIAN FOLK SONG

KIPPERED SALMON
page 146
SMOKED
STURGEON
HERRING
TIDBITS
HERRING
ROLLMOPS

BEET-CURED GRAVLAX
page 149
HOME-CURED LOX
page 143
SMOKED SABLE

HERRING
ROLLMOPS
page 141

WHAT'S A PARTY WITHOUT A PLATTER?

INTO EVERY JEWISH HOUSEHOLD, a few platters will be delivered. Shiva. Yom Kippur's break-fast. Tisha b'Av. Sunday brunch at the bride's parents' home. B'nai mitzvah weekends. In traditional communities, these platters are assembled at either the appetizing store or the delicatessen.

Appetizing shops offer milchig, or dairy, foods and smoked and pickled fishes, as well as parve foods like pickles and salads that fall into neither category—Russ & Daughters and Zabar's in New York are classic examples.

Delicatessens sell fleishig, or meat-based, foods like cured and smoked meats, knishes, and pickled tongue. Especially in America's early immigrant neighborhoods, meat and dairy were never commingled in the same shop.

Growing up, I saw only two types of platters, and they came from the appetizing store. There was the salad platter (Tuna, Egg, and Smoked Whitefish Salads; pages 158, 154, and 162), with pickled beets and Half Sour Pickles (page 169), generously decorated with curly parsley, black olives, and cherry tomatoes; and the fish platter, with Lox (page 143) and Kippered Salmon (page 146), herring, whitefish, sable, and sturgeon and mountains of plain and chive schmears (see pages 105 to 133). Fancy platters sometimes had red salmon roe, which I found fascinating and deliciously briny. Garnishes of red onion and cucumber slices, radish roses, capers, and lemon wedges were tucked in

Occasionally, for really large groups, there might be a platter from the delicatessen with corned beef and pastrami, sliced turkey, and beef salami, but that contradicts enough kasrut (kosher) laws that the introduction of these fleishig platters was a bold move and rare.

This chapter celebrates the appetizing of my childhood, which leaned heavily Ashkenazi with a touch of Lithuanian. In it, you'll find recipes for every element in a milchig appetizing platter—fishes, deli salads, and pickles—including several family favorites that are near and dear to my heart. I've become my Grandmother Mary with jars of Summer Beet Borscht (page 173) in my refrigerator, and I remember my Grandfather Allan when I slice sweet onions for Onions and Eggs (page 177). Use these recipes to create your own family memories.

ANATOMY OF AN APPETIZING PLATTER

FISHES

No platter is complete without a variety of fishes: Nova is cold-smoked salmon, velvety and salty-sweet. Smoked sturgeon is creamy and succulent. Sable is moist, tender, flaky, and tinged with light smoke. Pickled herring fillets with or without a cream sauce are a must. These are not the fish even the most intrepid of DIYers (usually) make at home.

It's actually a breeze to make lox in your own kitchen (see page 143), or to kipper (hot smoke) a piece of salmon (see page 146). For most of the other fishes, if you don't live near an appetizing store, there are talented purveyors who will ship right to your home. If you want to make your own platter, plan ahead and include some variety in the fishes.

SCHMEARING WITH THE FISHES

Salmon

Salmon will always win the day on a fish platter. Lox and belly lox are not smoked, only cured; the flesh is silky and melts on the tongue. Gravlax is the Scandinavian version of the Jewish lox: herbal, sweet, and salty, often tinged with alcohol, with no smoke at all. Nova is lightly cold-smoked, so it does not flake, but slices. It's sweet and salty, brightly colored and moist. Pastrami salmon is cured and cold-smoked, like Nova, with a crust of black pepper and coriander and a heavier smoke flavor. Kippered, or hot-smoked, salmon (sometimes called baked) is sweet, pale pink, and flaky.

Sturgeon

Sturgeon, a behemoth of a North Atlantic fish, can grow to 12 ft [3.7 m] in length. The largest ever to be fished weighed nearly 3,500 lb [1,588 kg], but more common are the 400 lb [181 kg] fish pulled from the cold waters. For centuries, these enormous fish, a source of healthful fats and oils, were smoked and preserved for winter sustenance. Smoked sturgeon is lightly flavored, smooth textured, and rich. It's my favorite smoked fish and the hardest to find.

Sable

Sable, sold as black cod on the West Coast, is another of the large-flaked, rich, fatty fish that is perfect for smoking and curing. It is often served in thick slabs to highlight the characteristic paprika-colored edge.

Smoked Whitefish

At 1½ to 2 lb [750 g to 1 kg] each, the lake whitefish has shiny gold skin and clear topaz eyes, and is sold head-and-tail whole. It has many bones, both large and small, and it takes some work to remove them (see Deboning a Whole Fish, page 160). Whitefish is tender and lightly flavored, its smoke resting on the tongue as the fish melts away. It is worth the work to serve with lemon wedges and sour cream or to mix it into Smoked Whitefish Salad (page 162).

Smoked Trout
Freshwater trout fillets, cured and lightly smoked, often sold (deboned) in a vacuum pack, are widely available in grocery stores. Trout fillets are smaller than other smoked fish, the right size for two or three people. When whitefish isn't easily available, I use trout as a stand-in in salads and dips.

Hot-Smoked Whiting
Whiting is a small, bony fish from fresh waters. It's brined and hot-smoked and has a stronger flavor than many of the other fish on the platter. It's generally served right off the bone.

Herring
Caught in weirs along the shallower, warmer edges of cold northern oceans, herring are easy to fish as they travel in schools, spawning several times a year. Harvested for centuries seasonally and in great quantities, they made a good storage fish, providing food all winter long. They can be consumed raw, pickled and cured, or smoked (as a kipper in the UK). Still, if I'm not visiting Scandanavia, I gravitate to the herring I know from my childhood, the familiar jars in the grocery store. Two or three pieces of herring and a few onions make a wonderful lunch with a toasted Pumpernickel Bagel (page 51).

I applaud those of you who pickle and preserve your own herring. I understand it's not difficult to do but sourcing fresh herring can be.

Herring and onions in a wine sauce are a common option, and herring in a cream sauce is sweet, velvety, and pickled at the same time. In herring-rich shops, look for rollmops, larger fillets rolled around a cucumber or onion pickle, and herring in other sauces like dill mustard and sweet tomato and curry.

SALADS

Salads are sandwich fillers and serve-with-a-scoop lunches. Smoked whitefish salad is the jewel in the crown of the salads. To make it yourself, find a fish and debone it. While that might be challenging, the end result is so sensational you will be wondering how soon you can do it again.

SOURS

No platter is complete without pickles. Quick Pickled Onions (page 166) up your sandwich game. You can make your own Half Sour Pickles (page 169) with three ingredients and a little time. Or, stir together Spicy Marinated Olives (page 172) for a decadent side or as an add-in for Olive Cheese (page 113).

BREADBASKET

Here's where we shine:
The breadbasket forms the foundation of the platter experience, and this is where bagels, bialys, and pletzels fit in. But feel free to add other flavors to your breadbasket outside of the recipes in this book too. My grandfather Ben wanted rye bread for his herring, never toasted. My grandmother Mary might snack on melba toast, a swipe of salted butter, and a slim nugget of Nova while setting up for company. Your breadbasket should suit your eaters and include whatever sounds delicious.

HOME-CURED LOX (CURED SALMON) SERVES 6

1 LB [500 G] SKIN-ON, CENTER-CUT SALMON FILLET

¼ CUP [50 G] GRANULATED SUGAR

¼ CUP [32 G] KOSHER SALT

TRADITIONAL LOX, OR CURED SALMON, is made with salmon belly, the thickest, fattiest part of the fish. A nice fat piece of salmon is glorious, but I'll cure any part of the salmon I'm given. If it's the thinner tail end, I simply plan for less time to achieve the silky, firm joy that is lox. Lox is never smoked, only cured in a simple mixture of salt and sugar where neither the salt nor the sugar should be noticeable. See Salt (page 22) to adjust the cure for different types of kosher salt.

1 Place a long sheet of aluminum foil on a clean work surface and cover it with a long sheet of plastic wrap. Set the salmon skin-side down on the plastic wrap. Inspect the salmon for any pin bones and use a pair of tweezers to remove them.

2 In a small bowl, combine the sugar and salt. Press the mixture into the flesh side of the salmon. Use the plastic wrap to snugly enclose the fillet, then double-wrap it with the foil.

3 Place the packet flat in a shallow glass or ceramic dish. Place another dish on top of the wrapped fish and add cans of tomatoes or jars of pickles or whatever weight will balance securely in the refrigerator and provide significant heft. (I keep a foil-wrapped masonry brick in the pantry and use it only for this purpose.)

4 After 24 hours, dispose of any juices that may have gathered in the bottom of the dish. Flip the fish packet over and reapply the weight.

5 Unwrap and check the fish after 48 hours; it should be firm all the way through. Press with your fingertips to check the thickest part of the fish to see if the texture has changed from tender to firm, raw to cured; there should be some resistance and the color will deepen. If it seems to need more time, rewrap it, flip it over, and replace the weight. Check again in 12 hours, and again 12 hours later, if needed. The fish will never take more than 72 hours to cure.

6 Unwrap the fish and brush away the salt-sugar mixture. The fish should be firm and deeply pink. Pat the fish with a paper towel to remove any remaining cure. Slice off a little of the lox to taste because you earned it.

7 Serve, thinly sliced (see How to Slice Cured Salmon, page 144), at room temperature or very slightly cold.

8 Lox will keep for 1 week in the refrigerator. I often slice and portion the fish, wrapping it tightly and freezing it in 2 oz [55 g] portions, just enough for a bagel. Defrost the lox in the refrigerator overnight and be rewarded at breakfast. Lox will keep for 3 months in the freezer.

HOW TO SLICE CURED SALMON

Place the fish, skin-side down, on a piece of paper towel on top of a cutting board; the towel will keep the fish from sliding around. Using a thin, flexible slicing knife, cut long, slim, translucent slices at the deepest angle possible. You should be able to read the newspaper through the slice, according to my grandfather Allan. Save any trimmings to add to scrambled eggs or stir into your homemade Lox Cheese (page 111).

KIPPERED, OR HOT-SMOKED, SALMON

SERVES 10

For the fish

2 LB [1 KG] SKIN-ON, CENTER-CUT SALMON FILLET

1 CUP [220 G] FIRMLY PACKED LIGHT BROWN SUGAR

5 TBSP [40 G] KOSHER OR SEA SALT

For the glaze

2 TBSP SOY SAUCE

2 TBSP GRANULATED SUGAR

KIPPERED SALMON IS SWEET, flaky, and scented with woodsmoke. On a fish platter, its chunky texture contrasts with the translucent lox or Nova. Smoking salmon is quick in an electric, pellet, or natural wood smoker, but it is also surprisingly easy to manage in the home kitchen, even in an apartment. Just note that good ventilation is imperative here (and be prepared to stop your smoke alarm's blare, just in case).

Shop for salmon with a high fat content—no coho or other lean versions—as hot-smoking will dry out the fish. This can be countered with a sweet brine, but if the fish is very lean, it will always end up dry. (On the bright side, even if it is very dry, it can make a great salmon salad. Just substitute the salmon for the tuna in Tuna Salad, page 158.) If you are shopping at a fish counter, ask for a single, center-cut piece.

1 To cure the fish, place a long sheet of aluminum foil on a clean work surface and cover it with a long sheet of plastic wrap. Set the salmon skin-side down on the plastic wrap. Inspect the salmon for any pin bones and use a pair of tweezers to remove them.

2 In a small bowl, combine the brown sugar and salt. Press this mixture over the flesh side of the salmon. Use the plastic wrap to snugly enclose the fish, then double-wrap it with the foil.

3 Place the packet flat in a shallow glass or ceramic dish. Place another dish on top of the wrapped fish and add cans of tomatoes or jars of pickles or whatever weight will balance securely in the refrigerator and provide significant heft. (I keep a foil-wrapped masonry brick in the pantry and use it only for this purpose.) CONT'D

4 After 24 hours, dispose of any juices that may have gathered in the bottom of the dish. Flip the fish packet over and reapply the weight.

5 Unwrap and check the fish after 48 hours; it should be firmer with a deeper color. Brush away the salt-sugar mixture and pat the fish well with a paper towel to remove any remaining cure. Place the fish skin-side down on a wire rack set over a baking sheet and refrigerate, uncovered, for 12 hours, to develop a tacky, dry exterior pellicle.

6 To make the glaze, whisk together the soy sauce and granulated sugar in a small bowl until the sugar has dissolved. Set aside.

7 To smoke on an outdoor smoker: Heat the outdoor smoker to 175°F [80°C] using alder or another mild-scented wood. Brush the flesh side of the fish with half of the glaze, reserving the rest.

8 Place the salmon skin-side down on a center rack or suspend it vertically from an upper rack. To suspend it, make a small hole in an outside corner of the fillet with a sharp knife. Push kitchen twine through the hole and use it to tie the fish to one of the racks in the smoker. Smoke to an internal temperature of 150°F [65°C], about 2 hours.

9 To smoke with an indoor smoker: Use a stovetop smoker, following the manufacturer's instructions, or use a heavy wok over high heat. Place a packet of wood chips wrapped in foil at the bottom of the wok. Place a cake rack in the wok, suspended over the chips. Set the salmon, skin-side down, on the rack. Brush with half of the glaze. Turn on the fan, open the windows, and cover the wok with foil.

10 Lift the edge of the foil and wait for the first sign of smoke to emerge, then tuck the foil around securely, and, if you have a heavy pot lid that is large enough, place it on top of the foil, making certain the foil does not touch the fish. This will further seal in the smoke. Smoke to an internal temperature of 150°F [65°C], about 25 minutes.

11 Once the fish emerges from whichever smoker you're using, brush it with the remaining glaze and serve.

12 Wrapped well, it will keep in the refrigerator for 1 week or in the freezer for 6 months.

BEET-CURED GRAVLAX

SERVES 8

- 8 OZ [225 G], RAW, RED BEETS, PEELED (ABOUT 2 MEDIUM)
- 1 LB [500 G] SKIN-ON, CENTER-CUT SALMON FILLET
- ¼ CUP [15 G] FRESH DILL, FINELY CHOPPED
- ¼ CUP [15 G] FRESH MINT, FINELY CHOPPED
- 2 TBSP GIN, VODKA, OR AQUAVIT
- ¼ CUP [50 G] GRANULATED SUGAR
- ¼ CUP [36 G] KOSHER SALT

GRAVLAX IS A FORM OF CURED SALMON that hails from Scandinavia. Naturally, because of geographic proximity, some traditions crossed borders, and Jews in northern Russia were also gravlax-ing. Here, salmon takes on the deep rose hue and sweet flavor of beets, laced with mint and dill. While lox uses a basic cure, gravlax offers a more nuanced flavor. Some of that comes from the addition of booze, particularly if you use a juniper-forward gin (if you are not a gin person, use vodka or the original, aquavit). Slice the magenta-edged fish very thin (see How to Slice Cured Salmon, page 144) and drape it over the schmear of your choice. The trimmings, after slicing, may be incorporated into the Lox Cheese (page 111) or the Hot-Smoked Salmon Cheese (page 112) or stirred into Allan Kadetsky's Onions and Eggs (page 177).

1 Using the medium holes on a hand grater or box grater, shred about 1 cup [150 g] of the beets. Set aside.

2 Place a long sheet of aluminum foil on a clean work surface and cover it with a long sheet of plastic wrap. Set the salmon skin-side down on the plastic wrap. Inspect the salmon for any pin bones and use a pair of tweezers to remove them.

3 Press the grated beets into the flesh side of the salmon. Top the beets with the finely chopped dill and mint, sprinkle with the gin, and spread the sugar and salt across the herbs. Use the plastic wrap to snugly enclose the fillet, then double-wrap with the foil.

4 Place the packet flat in a shallow glass or ceramic dish. Place another dish on top of the wrapped fish and add cans of tomatoes or jars of pickles or whatever weight will balance securely in the refrigerator and provide significant heft. (I keep a foil-wrapped masonry brick in the pantry and use it only for this purpose.) **CONT'D**

5 After 24 hours, dispose of any juices that may have gathered in the bottom of the dish. Flip the fish packet over and reapply the weight.

6 Unwrap and check the fish after 48 hours; it should be firm all the way through. Press with your fingertips to check the thickest part of the fish to see if the texture has changed from tender to firm, raw to cured; there should be some resistance.

7 Brush away all of the cure, herbs, and beets. The fish should be a glorious bright, deep pink. Rinse briefly in water and dry assiduously. Slice off a little piece to taste because you earned it. Serve very thinly sliced.

8 Wrapped well, gravlax will keep for 3 weeks in the refrigerator, or up to 6 months in the freezer.

BALABOOSTA MAYONNAISE

MAKES 1 CUP [230 G]

- 2 LARGE EGG YOLKS
- 3 TBSP FRESHLY SQUEEZED LEMON JUICE
- ½ TSP DIJON MUSTARD
- ¼ TSP KOSHER SALT
- ⅛ TSP GROUND WHITE PEPPER OR FRESHLY GROUND BLACK PEPPER
- ⅓ CUP [80 ML] OLIVE OIL
- ⅔ CUP [160 ML] GRAPESEED, SUNFLOWER, OR AVOCADO OIL

EVERY TIME I MAKE MAYONNAISE, I wonder why I don't do it more often. It's spectacularly delicious, creamy, and so different from what comes in the jar from the grocery store. Not that there's anything wrong with grocery store mayos—whether you side with Hellman's, a.k.a. Best Foods, or Duke's, they're all delicious in my mind. But when I do make mayonnaise from scratch, I realize it takes about five minutes and is decidedly better.

Whenever possible, use excellent eggs, the kind that come from backyard chickens or small farms where chickens freely forage.

1 Use a folded tea towel to make a nest on the counter for a medium mixing bowl. This will keep the bowl from sliding around.

2 Add the egg yolks, lemon juice, mustard, salt, and pepper to the bowl and whisk until the yolks are slightly lightened, 1 minute or so.

3 Combine the oils in a pitcher or measuring cup with a spout. Whisking constantly, drizzle the oils into the yolk mixture drop by drop. This process will take 3 or 4 minutes to emulsify the oils into the fats. When all the oil has been added, whisk the mayo a few times to combine, then taste, and correct for acidity (lemon juice), salt, or pepper.

4 Sealed in a container, the mayonnaise can be refrigerated for 2 days. Mayonnaise cannot be frozen.

BALABOOSTA SOUR CREAM

MAKES 16 OZ [240 G]

2 CUPS [475 ML] HEAVY CREAM, NOT ULTRA-PASTEURIZED

2 TBSP FRESH, CULTURED BUTTERMILK

SOUR CREAM is one of the most useful dairy products in the kitchen. It can stand in for heavy cream in most applications, binding deli salads (see pages 154 to 162) and lightening up cream cheese for schmears. I make sour cream when I have cream in the refrigerator that might go bad. Sour cream gives it new life. Use the best cream available; organic and from a local dairy is ideal. Allow 24 to 36 hours for culturing.

1 In a widemouthed jar with a lid, add the cream and buttermilk. Stir gently, loosely cover, and place in a cool spot (around 70°F [21°C]). Check the mixture after 24 hours; it should be thick and creamy and taste a little sour and tangy. If it is not firm enough, allow it to culture for an additional 4 to 6 hours. Tighten the lid on the jar and refrigerate. The sour cream will become firmer as it chills and will keep for 2 weeks in the refrigerator. To extend the sour cream's freshness, pour off any whey, the slightly opaque liquid that appears.

MAKE MINE CRÈME FRAÎCHE

Leave sour cream to culture for another 24 hours or so and voilà! It's crème fraîche. Really, it is that simple.

EGG SALAD

SERVES 4

1/4 CUP [55 G] BALABOOSTA MAYONNAISE (PAGE 152) OR STORE-BOUGHT

2 TBSP BALABOOSTA SOUR CREAM (PAGE 153) OR PLAIN YOGURT

2 TBSP SWEET PICKLE RELISH

1/2 TSP DIJON MUSTARD

1/4 TSP KOSHER SALT, PLUS MORE AS NEEDED

1/8 TSP FRESHLY GROUND BLACK PEPPER, PLUS MORE AS NEEDED

6 LARGE EGGS, HARD-BOILED, PEELED, AND CHOPPED

2 TBSP CHOPPED FRESH CHIVES

EGG SALAD is my way of making deviled eggs. Just kidding. But really. I hate peeling hard-boiled eggs, and no matter how many times I try and how many solutions for easing the peeling, a few of the boiled eggs get shredded. Turn to egg salad, where the quality of your peeling won't come into question. Chop the eggs into small pieces about the size of a pea, because large chunks will slip off the bagel and make a mess of your shirt.

1 In a medium bowl, combine the mayonnaise, sour cream, relish, mustard, salt, and pepper. Gently fold the chopped eggs into the mayonnaise mixture using a flexible spatula. Sprinkle the chives over the surface and stir again. Cover and chill for about 1 hour before serving. Taste and correct for salt and pepper, as needed.

2 Covered, the egg salad will keep for 3 days in the refrigerator.

PLEASING MAYO HATERS

For some people, mayonnaise is anathema: Never shall it pass their lips. For the mayo-denying types, there is no substitute that will make a deli salad appealing. But for those who remain open to a creamy salad, I offer these options.

CRÈME FRAÎCHE OR SOUR CREAM (see Balaboosta Sour Cream, page 153) plus lemon juice will mimic the creamy binding of mayonnaise as well as the bright acidic snap.

PLAIN YOGURT, DRAINED OR GREEK-STYLE, will bind less, making for a looser salad, but it brings the tang.

SILKEN TOFU PLUS LEMON JUICE will whisk together into a slightly thicker binder. It will need some salt.

SMALL-CURD, LOW-FAT COTTAGE CHEESE plus a spoonful of sour cream plus lemon juice is a way to get the binding, the tang, and the delicious texture without the calories. Whip this combination together with a whisk.

CHICKEN SALAD

SERVES 4

For the chicken

- 1 LB [500 G] BONELESS, SKINLESS CHICKEN BREASTS (ABOUT 3 HALVES)
- ½ CUP [120 ML] BUTTERMILK
- 1 CUP [235 ML] COOL WATER
- 1 TSP KOSHER SALT
- 4 OR 5 SPRIGS FRESH THYME
- 1 BAY LEAF

For the dressing

- ¼ CUP [65 G] PLAIN YOGURT
- 2 TBSP BALABOOSTA MAYONNAISE (PAGE 152) OR STORE-BOUGHT
- 2 TBSP CAPERS PLUS 1 TSP CAPER BRINE
- ½ TSP DIJON MUSTARD
- ¼ CUP [55 G] CHOPPED CELERY
- 2 TBSP SLICED SCALLIONS
- ½ TSP FRESH THYME LEAVES
- ¾ TO 1 TSP KOSHER SALT
- ¼ TSP FRESHLY GROUND BLACK PEPPER

I LIKE POACHING CHICKEN BREASTS IN BUTTERMILK; it's acidic, which tenderizes the chicken, and adds less flavor than wine and more than plain water. After poaching, there will be a few curds from the buttermilk clinging to the chicken; either incorporate them into the salad or brush them away. Or forgo poaching and use leftover roast chicken.

1 To make the chicken, place the chicken and buttermilk in a large skillet with straight sides. Turn the chicken several times to coat in the buttermilk and set aside for 30 minutes.

2 Place the skillet over medium-high heat. Add the water, salt, thyme, and bay leaf to the skillet and bring to a boil. Lower the heat to low, cover, and simmer until a finger pressed into the chicken finds resistance, about 15 minutes. Use tongs to transfer the chicken to a cutting board. Discard the poaching liquid. When the chicken is cool to the touch, chop into small pieces about the size of chickpeas.

3 To make the dressing, in a medium bowl, combine the yogurt, mayonnaise, capers, caper brine, mustard, celery, scallions, thyme, salt, and pepper. Gently fold the chicken into the dressing using a flexible spatula. Cover and chill for about 1 hour before serving.

4 Covered, the chicken salad will keep for 3 days in the refrigerator.

TUNA SALAD

SERVES 4

2 JARS (EACH 7.7 OZ [220 G]) WHITE TUNA IN OLIVE OIL, DRAINED

SCANT ½ CUP [115 G] BALABOOSTA MAYONNAISE (PAGE 152) OR STORE-BOUGHT

⅓ CUP [65 G] FINELY CHOPPED CELERY

2 TBSP LEMON JUICE, PLUS MORE AS NEEDED

2 TBSP CHOPPED PARSLEY

1 TSP JARRED HORSERADISH, PLUS MORE AS NEEDED

¼ TSP KOSHER SALT, PLUS MORE AS NEEDED

⅛ TSP FRESHLY GROUND BLACK PEPPER, PLUS MORE AS NEEDED

GIVE ME TUNA SALAD with crunch and a bite. Add a nice big spoonful of horseradish (I like a lot), plenty of lemon juice, and tiny pieces of crisp celery. Sometimes I add a hard-boiled egg or two. Most importantly, find imported tuna packed in jars, in olive oil. It's more flavorful by far.

For a classic ladies' lunch, fill a hollowed-out tomato half with tuna salad and serve it with bagel chips (see page 40) on the side. Or pile the tuna salad on a halved bagel, drape a piece of American cheese over the top, and broil it for the best tuna melt ever.

1 In a medium bowl, flake the tuna with a fork. In another bowl, combine the mayonnaise, celery, lemon juice, parsley, horseradish, salt, and pepper. Gently fold the tuna into the wet ingredients using a silicone spatula or a fork, leaving some of the tuna chunky. Cover and chill for about 1 hour before serving. Taste and correct for lemon, salt, and pepper, as needed.

2 Covered, the tuna salad will keep for 3 days in the refrigerator, but it tastes best the first day.

SMOKED
WHITEFISH SALAD
page 162
SMOKED
TROUT SPREAD
page 163
TUNA SALAD
page 158

DEBONING A WHOLE FISH

Step 1

TAKE NOTE

Have a serving platter close by. Take a moment to review the fish. Notice the backbone (vertebrae) along the top of the fish. From the vertebrae, on each side of the fish, look for two sets of bones: spine bones and pin bones.

Step 2

OPEN THE FISH

Remove the head and tail with a sharp chef's knife, slicing straight down. Use scissors to cut away the two fins.

With the backbone-side down, open the fish like a book. From the inside, press along each side of the vertebrae gently, pushing the flesh down and away from the skeleton without splitting or cracking any bones along the way. The goal is to free the flesh.

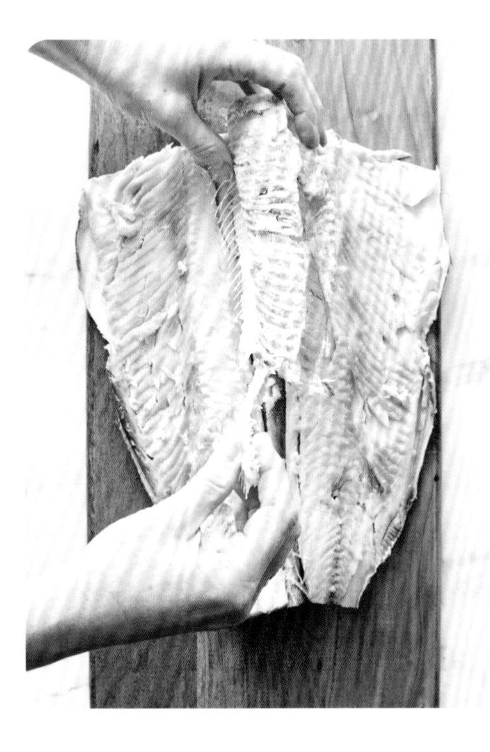

Step 3

REMOVE THE BONES

Starting at the tail end, pull up and remove the backbone, taking with it as many spine and pin bones as possible. Work slowly and meticulously for the best result.

A hard skin encases the rib bones and sits atop the flesh along the belly; use the flat side of a paring knife to gently ease that skin and the rib bones away from the fish to reveal the fillet on each side.

Step 4

EXTRACT THE FILLETS AND SERVE

Gently remove the fillets of belly meat and place them on the platter. Use your fingers to check and double-check for and remove any remaining pin bones from the fillets on the platter. They are small and mighty.

Decorate the plate with parsley and lemon slices. Shower the fish with capers and finely minced red onion. Serve with sour cream on the side.

SMOKED WHITEFISH SALAD

SERVES 8

1 WHOLE SMOKED WHITEFISH (1½ TO 2 LB [750 G TO 1 KG]), SKINNED, BONED, AND FLAKED (YIELDING APPROXIMATELY 3 CUPS, OR 1 LB [500 G])

1 CUP [240 G] BALABOOSTA SOUR CREAM (PAGE 153) OR STORE-BOUGHT

½ CUP [115 G] FINELY CHOPPED CELERY

¼ CUP [15 G] CHOPPED CHIVES OR FINELY MINCED SCALLIONS

1 TBSP JARRED HORSERADISH

JUICE OF 1 LEMON (ABOUT ¼ CUP [60 ML]), PLUS MORE AS NEEDED

½ TSP KOSHER SALT, PLUS MORE AS NEEDED

¼ TSP FRESHLY GROUND BLACK PEPPER, PLUS MORE AS NEEDED

WHEN I WAS GROWING UP, smoked whitefish was an essential part of every Sunday bagel brunch, and Nova or belly lox was reserved for parties and special occasions. While there is an actual lake whitefish, the term *whitefish* has come to refer to any mild-flavored freshwater fish with small bones and moist, fatty flesh. In Minnesota and many other Midwestern states, smoked whitefish is common and found in the supermarket, while in other places (like my current hometown), whitefish is an hour away. Smoked whitefish salad takes work, and there's no making half the recipe. See Deboning a Whole Fish (page 160) for how to extract the flesh and leave the bones behind.

For a real treat, try making it with half whitefish and half Kippered, or Hot-Smoked, Salmon (page 146). If you are not a fan of celery, try finely chopped fennel or seeded cucumber—the crunch is imperative. Just note that these substitutions will give your salad a shorter shelf life.

1 Place the flaked fish in a large bowl and carefully pick through to locate and dispose of any tiny bones. Gently stir in the sour cream, celery, chives, horseradish, lemon juice, salt, and pepper. Chill for 30 minutes before serving. Taste and adjust the lemon juice, salt, and pepper as needed.

2 Covered, the whitefish salad will keep for 4 days in the refrigerator. It cannot be frozen.

SMOKED TROUT SPREAD

SERVES 4 AS AN APPETIZER

- 4 TBSP [55 G] BALABOOSTA CREAM CHEESE (PAGE 103) OR STORE-BOUGHT, SOFTENED
- 2 TBSP [30 G] SALTED BUTTER, SOFTENED
- 2 TBSP FINELY CHOPPED CHIVES
- 1 TSP JARRED HORSERADISH
- ½ TSP DIJON MUSTARD
- ½ TSP FRESH THYME LEAVES
- ⅓ LB [170 G] SMOKED TROUT, BONED AND SKINNED

WHEN WHITEFISH IS NOWHERE TO BE FOUND, I turn to smoked trout for a smoky freshwater fish treat. While it doesn't have quite the same texture and unctuousness as whitefish, trout is similarly mild and carries a smokier flavor. This recipe is more spread than salad, along the lines of a French rillette. I like the variation in texture it offers on a platter full of classic spreads. It's delicious served on a cucumber round, watermelon radish slice, or bagel chip (see page 40) at cocktail hour. Top deviled eggs with a rosette of smoked trout spread or up your avocado toast game by adding it as an underlying layer. For a change of pace, substitute smoked Nova salmon for half of the trout.

1 In a medium bowl, use a stiff spatula to combine the cream cheese, butter, chives, horseradish, mustard, and thyme. Add the trout and use a fork to break it up into small pieces. Stir until the spread is a consistent texture with no large clumps of fish. Pack the spread into a ramekin or two, cover, and chill for at least an hour. Let warm slightly before serving.

2 The smoked trout spread will keep for 3 days in the refrigerator. It cannot be frozen.

CARROT PINEAPPLE SALAD

SERVES 4

- 8 OZ [225 G] CARROTS, GRATED (ABOUT 2 CUPS, FROM 3 TO 5 MEDIUM CARROTS)
- ¼ CUP [65 G] PLAIN YOGURT
- ¼ CUP [55 G] DICED PINEAPPLE, DRAINED (IF USING CANNED)
- ¼ CUP [40 G] DRIED CURRANTS
- 2 TBSP CHOPPED PARSLEY
- 1 TBSP PLUS 1½ TSP FINELY DICED RED ONION
- 1 TBSP APPLE CIDER VINEGAR
- ¼ TSP KOSHER SALT, PLUS MORE AS NEEDED
- ⅛ TSP FRESHLY GROUND BLACK PEPPER, PLUS MORE AS NEEDED

THE PARKWAY DELI in my old DC neighborhood has a legendary pickle bar. The half sours and full sours join pickled beets, hot peppers, sauerkraut, pickled eggs, and more. For me, the biggest draw is the carrot salad—sweet, creamy, and tart—with pineapple, chewy raisins, and a little onion bite.

In this recipe, I've replaced raisins with currants because I like the size better, but raisins or even dried cranberries are able substitutes. The carrots will need to wilt a little but still retain some tooth and should never ever be mushy. The dressing may seem skimpy, but it is not.

I prefer to shred the carrots in a food processor fitted with a grating disk, but the same texture can be achieved with the medium holes on a box grater. Or get fancy and finely julienne the carrots with a mandoline. Use fresh or canned diced pineapple interchangeably.

1 Place the shredded carrots in a medium bowl and add the yogurt, pineapple, currants, parsley, red onion, vinegar, salt, and pepper. Stir together until combined. Cover and refrigerate for 1 hour before serving. Stir again and adjust the salt or pepper as needed.

2 Covered, the carrot salad will keep for 3 days in the refrigerator. It cannot be frozen.

QUICK PICKLED ONIONS

MAKES 2 CUPS [ABOUT 200 G DRAINED]

1½ CUPS [230 G] THINLY SLICED RED ONION (SLICED INTO HALF-MOONS)

¾ CUP [175 ML] APPLE CIDER VINEGAR

¾ CUP [175 ML] WATER

1½ TSP PICKLING SPICE

¾ TSP KOSHER SALT

⅛ TSP CRUSHED RED PEPPER

PICKLED RED ONIONS are the tangy condiment I can't live without. It's fortunate they take only a few minutes to make. Never let another half onion go bad in the vegetable drawer: Pickle it! In this case, the pickling is very mild, less a pucker-pickle and more an onion with less of a bite. Pile them on grain salads, scrambled eggs, sandwiches, and barbecued meats, and naturally, serve alongside bagels and lox.

1 Place the onion slices in a small glass or ceramic bowl or a widemouthed 1 pt [480 ml] jar.

2 In a small saucepan over medium-high heat, bring the vinegar, water, pickling spice, salt, and crushed red pepper to a slight boil. Stir to dissolve the salt, remove from the heat, and pour the hot brine over the onions. Set aside, uncovered, for 20 minutes.

3 At this point, the onions are ready to serve, though will likely still be warm. If you prefer them chilled but are rushing to the table, use an ice-water bath: Just fit the smaller bowl of onions and brine into a larger bowl of ice water. Stir the onions until the brine has chilled.

4 The onions will keep, covered, for 1 month in the refrigerator.

QUICK PICKLED ONIONS
page 166

QUICK PICKLED
CARROTS
page 168

QUICK PICKLED CARROTS

MAKES ONE 1 QT [1 L] JAR

- 1 LB [500 G] SLIM YOUNG CARROTS, SCRUBBED AND PEELED (8 TO 10 CARROTS)
- 2 TSP CELERY SEEDS
- 1 TSP JUNIPER BERRIES
- 1 JALAPEÑO, STEMMED, SEEDED, AND HALVED, OPTIONAL
- 1 CUP [235 ML] APPLE CIDER VINEGAR
- 1 CUP [235 ML] WATER
- ¼ CUP [50 G] SUGAR
- ¼ CUP [32 G] KOSHER SALT
- 1 GARLIC CLOVE, PEELED

YOUNG CARROTS are sweet and tender. As they grow larger and are stored longer, the flavor becomes more rugged. For this pickle, look for young carrots so the sweetness carries over to the pickle. The juniper brine is bright and tangy and a great foil to cured fish. Include the jalapeño if you like it spicy. These carrots make an excellent and colorful garnish in a gin and tonic.

1 Fill a large bowl with ice water. Place the carrots in a single layer in a skillet. Cover with water and bring to a boil over medium-high heat. Cook the carrots until just tender (a knife tip will slip in with a little resistance), about 3 minutes. Transfer the carrots to the ice water bath to stop the cooking.

2 Fit the carrots into a 1 qt [1 L] jar. If they are too tall, cut in half horizontally and stand those pieces in the jar. Spoon the celery seeds and juniper berries into the jar. Add the jalapeño, if using.

3 In a small saucepan over medium-high heat, bring the vinegar, water, sugar, salt, and garlic to a boil, stirring to dissolve the salt and sugar. Pour the hot brine over the carrots to fill the jar. Discard any leftover brine.

4 Let cool, seal the jar with its lid, and leave on the counter overnight to brine. Transfer to the refrigerator.

5 The pickled carrots will keep for 1 week in the refrigerator.

HALF AND FULL SOUR PICKLES

MAKES TWO 1 QT [1 L] JARS

2 LB [1 KG] FRESHLY PICKED PICKLING CUCUMBERS

2 DILL FLOWERS OR 2 TSP DILL SEED

4 CUPS [1 L] WATER (SEE HEADNOTE)

2 TBSP KOSHER SALT

2 LARGE GARLIC CLOVES

WHEN I WAS A CHILD, a trip to the deli meant pickles for me. It delighted the deli man, Mr. Breuer, that I could singlehandedly eat an entire bowl of pickled cucumbers from half to wholly sour.

To make a deli pickle, all it takes is a simple, salty brine and time to ferment. Leave the pickles in the salt brine longer for a serious pucker. This pickle only works with a pickling cucumber, often called Kirby, usually harvested early in the summer and again in the latter part of the growing season. They are found year-round at many Asian markets, but the more freshly picked, the firmer the cucumber and the less likely the pickle will turn mushy. I shop the farmers' market for the cukes with dirt still in the ridges. I like smaller ones because more fit in the jar.

Fermenting demands clear, clean water. If you have bottled water, use it. Or leave tap water out overnight so the chlorine can disperse. Fermentation times change when the kitchen is warm, so watch and taste to find the pickle that's the right level of sour for you.

1 Wash and dry two 1 qt [1 L] jars with lids.

2 Fill a large bowl with ice water and add the cucumbers, soaking and scrubbing them to loosen any dirt. With a sharp knife, slice off just the blossom end of each one (the opposite end from the stem). If you can't decide which end is which, slice a small amount off each.

3 Cut the cucumbers into halves, spears, or 1 in [2.5 cm] chunks, if you wish, or pickle them whole. Slice at least one of the cucumbers into chunks to use as the test pickle. Divide the dill flowers between the jars, then pack the cucumbers into the jars snugly. Place the test chunks on top for easy access. CONT'D

4 In a medium saucepan over high heat, combine 2 cups [475 ml] of the water with the salt and garlic cloves and bring to a boil, stirring to dissolve the salt. Remove the pan from the heat and, to speed the cooling process, add the remaining 2 cups [475 ml] of water, stirring to combine. Set aside to cool. Do not proceed with the recipe until the brine has cooled completely, about 30 minutes. Alternatively, quickly chill it by using an ice bath or refrigerating the brine.

5 Funnel the brine into the jars, making sure the pickles are submerged. (Any parts that are exposed will mold.) Place one garlic clove from the brine into each jar. Loosely cap the jars and place them on a baking sheet or in another pan; the jars may leak during fermentation. Discard any leftover brine.

6 Leave the pickles on the counter to ferment. The brine will bubble lazily and become cloudy. There may be some white foam that gathers at the surface. This is fine and safe and can be skimmed off. (If the foam is pink or purple, however, discard the contents and try again.) Fermentation may take 12 hours to 4 days, depending on the size of the cucumbers and the temperature in the kitchen.

7 Taste a test pickle after 1 day, and then again the next day, and so on. When the sourness and crispness are to your personal liking, seal the jars and refrigerate.

8 The pickles will keep for about 1 month in the refrigerator.

SPICY MARINATED OLIVES
page 172

HALF AND FULL SOUR PICKLES
page 169

SPICY MARINATED OLIVES

MAKES 1½ CUPS [195 G]

1½ CUPS [195 G] MIXED OLIVES, PITTED

½ CUP [120 ML] OLIVE OIL

1 ORANGE

3 SPRIGS FRESH OREGANO OR
½ TSP DRIED OREGANO

½ TSP CRUSHED RED PEPPER

THESE ZIPPY OLIVES are delicious as a cocktail hour snack alongside the Tamari Almonds (page 133) and spectacular in the Olive Cheese (page 113).

1 Rinse the olives in a colander and set aside.

2 Pour the olive oil into a medium bowl. Using a vegetable peeler, remove 3 swaths of orange peel, leaving the white pith behind. Add the peels to the bowl along with the juice of the orange, the oregano, and crushed red pepper. Whisk to combine. Add the olives and transfer the mixture to a glass jar with a lid.

3 Cover and let the olives marinate on the counter for 3 hours, then refrigerate.

4 The olives will keep for 2 weeks in the refrigerator.

SUMMER BEET BORSCHT

MAKES 4 CUPS [1 L]

1 LB [500 G] DARK RED BEETS, SCRUBBED CLEAN IF FRESH

4 CUPS [1 L] WATER, PLUS MORE AS NEEDED

1 TBSP KOSHER SALT, PLUS MORE AS NEEDED

¼ CUP [60 ML] LEMON JUICE OR APPLE CIDER VINEGAR

3 TBSP SUGAR

1 CUP [120 G] SEEDED AND DICED CUCUMBER, FOR GARNISH

½ CUP [113 G] BALABOOSTA SOUR CREAM (PAGE 153) OR STORE-BOUGHT, FOR GARNISH

FRESH SNIPPED CHIVES, FOR GARNISH

RELIABLY, EVERY SUMMER DAY of my childhood, I would spy two jars in my grandmother Mary's refrigerator. Each held cold borscht, one beet and one spinach (see Cold Spinach Borscht, page 176). She believed summer lunch should start with a refreshing glass or sipping bowl of soup. I was all in, blissfully unaware that this was unusual in mid-century American suburbs.

Mary used canned beets (two 13 oz [370 g] cans or jars of diced "Harvard" beets, to be precise). She was vain about her manicure and would never cut up a fresh beet. You can use fresh or canned, I won't tell. If using fresh beets, disposable kitchen gloves will protect your fingers from staining. While some borscht is served with the sour cream stirred in, Mary served it dolloped on top.

1 If using fresh beets, place the beets in a medium saucepan and add the water and salt. Set over high heat and bring to a boil, then lower the heat to medium, cover, and simmer the beets until tender, about 30 minutes (depending on size).

2 Remove the beets from the cooking liquid and let cool on a cutting board. Strain the cooking liquid through a double layer of cheesecloth or through a coffee filter, then measure how much liquid is left and add enough water to total 4 cups [1 L]. Return all that liquid to the pot. CONT'D

3 Peel the cooled beets, then dice or finely julienne them and return them to the liquid in the pot. Add the lemon juice and sugar. Heat through over medium heat until the sugar has dissolved.

4 If using canned beets, set the beets in a colander, capturing the liquid in a bowl below. Dice or finely julienne the beets and place in a medium saucepan. Strain the liquid again, this time through a double layer of cheesecloth, then measure how much liquid is left and add enough water to total 4 cups [1 L]. Pour the liquid over the beets, turn the heat to medium-high, and bring to a boil. Lower the heat to maintain a simmer, add the lemon juice and sugar, and heat until the sugar has dissolved.

5 Taste and correct for salt. Transfer the borscht to a lidded jar and refrigerate for at least 2 hours.

6 Serve chilled, garnished with diced cucumber, sour cream, and chives. The borscht will keep in the refrigerator for 1 week. It does not freeze.

COLD SPINACH
BORSCHT
page 176
SUMMER BEET
BORSCHT
page 173

COLD SPINACH BORSCHT (SCHAV)

MAKES 4 CUPS [1 L]

1 LB [500 G] FRESH SPINACH OR SORREL LEAVES (2 PACKED CUPS)

3 CUPS [710 ML] COLD WATER

½ CUP [120 ML] WHOLE MILK

1 LARGE EGG

1½ TSP SALT

JUICE OF ½ LEMON

⅓ CUP [75 G] BALABOOSTA SOUR CREAM (PAGE 153) OR STORE-BOUGHT

MY GRANDMOTHER MARY would hand out glasses of this cold soup, and because we were kids, we didn't know it was unusual to drink cold spinach soup—we just thought it was delicious. As I researched, I found dozens of soups called *schav* from Ukraine, Lithuania, Russia, and other northern climates. They were made with sturdy greens of any sort, but most often sorrel, a vigorous garden green, so lemony and fresh that it makes a cold soup sing. My grandmother's humble spinach soup is absolutely spectacular when made with sorrel, so if you find it at the market, try it as the centerpiece here. Whether you use spinach or sorrel, make sure to wash the greens well so the soup is not at all gritty, and serve the schav icy cold.

1 Fill a medium saucepan with the spinach and water. Turn the heat to high and bring to a boil. Remove from the heat and cover the pan for 2 to 4 minutes, until the greens have wilted but remain a bright green. Pour the water and greens into a blender, remove the center cap from the blender lid so steam can escape, and pulse, puréeing until nearly smooth. Return the mixture to the saucepan and bring back to a boil over medium-high heat, then remove from the heat.

2 Combine the milk, egg, and salt in a small bowl, whisking until no streaks of egg remain. Using a whisk, create a whirlpool in the center of the greens and, whisking continuously, slowly pour in the egg mixture. Return to a boil, remove from the heat, stir in the lemon juice, cover, and cool completely.

3 When the schav is completely cool, whisk in the sour cream. Pour into a 1 qt [1 L] jar and chill thoroughly. Taste and adjust for salt.

4 Shake before serving.The soup will keep for 3 days in the refrigerator. It should not be frozen.

ALLAN KADETSKY'S ONIONS AND EGGS

SERVES 8

4 TBSP [55 G] UNSALTED BUTTER

1 LB [500 G] LARGE VIDALIA OR SWEET ONIONS, SLICED INTO HALF-MOONS (ABOUT 3 PACKED CUPS)

1 TSP KOSHER SALT, PLUS MORE AS NEEDED

12 LARGE EGGS

⅓ CUP [79 ML] WHOLE MILK

½ TSP FRESHLY GROUND BLACK PEPPER, PLUS MORE AS NEEDED

SLOW-AND-LOW, LONG-COOKED, sweet onions have no pungency at all. My grandfather Allan's onions and eggs were legendary, and part of the fun was pestering him while he stirred the pot. Brunch was excruciatingly delayed, especially for a six-year-old, but once those delicate scrambled onions and eggs were on my plate, I couldn't get enough of them. Do your best to leave the onions alone, letting them soften and sweeten and become the best onions they can be. The Kadetskys used this time to enjoy Bloody Marys.

1 In a large, wide skillet over medium heat, melt the butter until foaming. Add the onions and ½ tsp of the salt, stir well, lower the heat to low, and leave the onions to wilt and sweeten, stirring from time to time. They are not supposed to be caramelized, but very slightly golden, tender, and wilted. This process should take about 1 hour.

2 In a large bowl, whisk together the eggs, milk, the remaining ½ tsp of salt, and the pepper until smooth and combined. Keeping the heat low, pour the eggs over the onions and stir with a silicone spatula or wooden spoon until large and fluffy curds form, no more than 4 or 5 minutes. Season with more salt or pepper, as needed, to support the soft, tender, oniony goodness. Serve when they are still quite custardy, moist, and piping hot.

BAGEL SANDW

CHES & SALADS

AN ITALIAN HERO BAGEL
page 192

THE BEC BAGEL
page 185

THANKSGIVING ANY DAY
page 191

PAN BAGELNAT
page 190

WAKE ME UP WITH A NECTARINE, BACON, AND JALAPEÑO BAGEL
page 186

IF A BAGEL WERE A BURRITO
page 187

SECRETS FOR BETTER SANDWICHING

THERE'S NO DENYING that bagel sandwiches can be challenging to eat. The best delis make bagel sandwiches that stay together. Where every bite includes every element. Where the type of bagel pairs perfectly with what's stacked between the two halves. You've made the bagel, you've fermented the pickle. You're ready to make a bagel sandwich like a pro.

Sliding and squishing are the enemies of eating a bagel sandwich, and the sheer ratio of bready exterior to stacked fillings has the potential to overwhelm. Layering the meats and condiments or tomatoes must be precise and specific. Slippery condiments contribute to increased laundry. Bagels are stiff, which makes them ideal for sandwiches made in the morning and consumed at noon, but that sturdy exterior shell also means a too-tall sandwich. As my friend Abbie says, "It's no problem. I'll just unhinge my jaw like a snake." I have solutions.

Scooping (more on this shortly), toasting, and the world of the open-face sandwich inform the bagel sandwich's architecture (hello Denmark and your smörgåsbord and France with your tartines). In the sandwich recipes that follow, I've employed these techniques to make bagel sandwiches easier to eat.

It's disheartening mid-bite to have the filling slide out from a bagel sandwich into your lap. To help avoid this messy moment, I like to scoop out some of the bagel's insides and use its emptied space to trap messy condiments or slippery sauces.

Sliced cheese has a tendency to slip too, and that's never good. When cheese is involved, let it meet a warm egg so it melts a little and sticks. Or run that cheese-draped, open-faced beauty under the broiler for a bubbling, freckled surface and toasty cheese goodness.

To stop the squish of fruit or vegetables slices, anchor them between greens or meat and use a condiment to glue everything in place.

The act of scooping, or removing the bready center from a split bagel, first started during the Carb Craze of the 1990s. Since then, for calorie counters and the carb-averse, it's de rigueur. And for some others, it's a reason to side-eye and declare the act an abomination. I've learned that a scooped bagel makes a tidy sandwich that's less likely to slide apart than a non-scooped bagel. And I'm going to leave it at that.

To remove the center portion of the bagel, first split it, then use a grapefruit spoon or a melon baller to scoop the center crumb away from the firm shell. The center portion can be toasted and ground in a blender for bread crumbs.

The following sandwiches and salads are simply a jumping-off point. Now that you have bagels in the house, have fun creating your own.

MAKE THE PERFECT BAGEL SANDWICH

OPT 1.

Press Down

Wrap the sandwich tightly, then gently compress the sandwich to blend the flavors. A bagel sandwich packed in the morning will be less soggy at lunchtime than a sandwich made with bread.

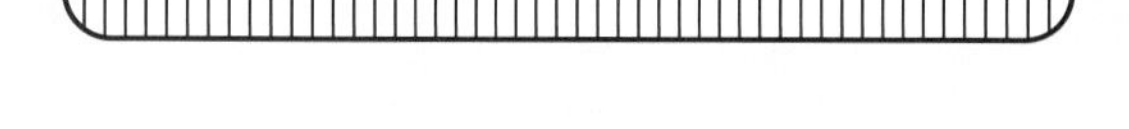

OPT 2.

Steam It

If the bagel is stale, emulate the signature Steamwich from the Chicago Bagel Authority. Place the fully formed bagel sandwich in a steamer basket (I like bamboo steamers) over barely simmering water. Press down on the sandwich. Cover, steam for 30 seconds, and enjoy the soft, tender bagel sandwich that emerges.

HOW DOES ONE SPREAD CREAM CHEESE ON A BAGEL?

Dear Miss Manners,

Assuming the bagel is cut in half, does one spread cream cheese on an entire half of the bagel? Or is a bagel treated as, say, a dinner roll, where one only butters the pieces that one breaks off?

I'm afraid that my family didn't come across bagels in the old country, so this has us a little mystified. (I admit I have been treating it as dinner bread—It seems less gauche than buttering an entire half-bagel.)

I await your answer with bated breath. There's a very nice bagel shop across the street, and I will enjoy it so much more when I know how to eat the bagels properly.

Gentle Reader,

Either method you describe is indeed proper, depending on whether you consider it a piece of bread or a sandwich.

However, Miss Manners warns you: Before you enjoy the bagels from across the street, make sure that you specify that they be delivered to you dry and/or whole. Otherwise, the shop will generally do the spreading for you, leaving you with a warm, cream cheesy gloop that will be nearly impossible to eat neatly—or to get off of your sleeve.

—From Miss Manners (syndicated) by
Judith Martin, Nicholas Ivor Martin, and Jacobina Martin

THE BACON EGG CHEESE (BEC) BAGEL

Makes 2 sandwiches

4 LARGE EGGS

2 TBSP WHOLE MILK

1 TBSP CHOPPED CHIVES

¼ TSP KOSHER SALT

⅛ TSP FRESHLY GROUND BLACK PEPPER

2 TBSP UNSALTED BUTTER

2 BAGELS, YOUR FAVORITE TYPE, SPLIT; TOASTING OPTIONAL

2 SLICES AMERICAN CHEESE

4 SLICES CRISPED BACON (4 OZ [112 G])

HOT SAUCE, OPTIONAL

I can't remember a trip to New York City that didn't involve at least one BEC breakfast, grabbed at the corner market and eaten on the run. I've been traveling less, so now I make them at home. The eggs are baked in a baking pan, which makes it easy to cut the fluffy scramble into stable portions that fit on the bagel. If I miss the joy of a trip to the city, I wrap my BEC in foil and eat it standing up.

If you have a mind to go over the top, a sizzling-hot latke (or crisped hash brown square) slipped in between the egg and the cheese adds just the right crunchy, salty bite to the rest of this beautiful sandwich.

Preheat the oven to 350°F [180°C]. Lightly coat a 9 by 4 in [23 by 10 cm] loaf pan with cooking spray, line it with parchment paper (allowing some overhang), and spray the paper. Place the eggs, milk, chives, salt, and pepper in a blender and mix on high speed until combined and frothy.

Pour the mixture into the prepared loaf pan and gently tap it on the counter to remove some of the air bubbles. Bake for 20 to 24 minutes, until cooked through but not dry.

Let the eggs cool slightly and remove them from the pan by lifting the parchment paper. Portion the eggs into two pieces, each about 4½ by 4 in [11 by 10 cm].

Butter the cut sides of the bagel halves. On the bottom half of each bagel, place a slice of cheese. Cover with a portion of the warm egg. Let it sit for a moment to melt the cheese a little, then top each sandwich with 2 slices of bacon, broken into pieces to fit.

Drizzle with hot sauce, if using. Top with the other half of the bagel, press down slightly, cut in half vertically, and serve.

WAKE ME UP WITH A NECTARINE, BACON, AND JALAPEÑO BAGEL

Makes 2 sandwiches

4 OZ [112 G] SCHMEAR MASTER RECIPE (PAGE 105)

2 MONTREAL-STYLE SESAME BAGELS (PAGE 45), SPLIT, SCOOPED (SEE PAGE 183), AND LIGHTLY TOASTED

1 PERFECTLY RIPE NECTARINE, HALVED, PITTED, AND THINLY SLICED

4 TO 8 THINLY SLICED ROUNDS JALAPEÑO PEPPER

4 SLICES CRISPED BACON, HALVED (4 OZ [112 G])

This sandwich, or a very close approximation, is offered at Call Your Mother, my favorite Washington, DC, bagel shop. There, the chefs swap in seasonal fruit throughout the year, but I had a sandwich with nectarine and can't kick it. The combo is likely to surprise you—salty, sweet, spicy, the textures, and the tang. From the very first bite, I was a believer, and I think you will be too.

Spread the schmear into the scooped tunnels of all four bagel halves. Divide and decoratively arrange the nectarine slices across the bottom half of each bagel, then tuck in the jalapeño slices. Add 2 slices of bacon to each bagel and top with the remaining bagel halves. Press down slightly, cut in half vertically, and serve.

NOSHING WITH THE FISHES

Makes 2 open-faced sandwiches

1 TBSP SALTED EUROPEAN BUTTER, SOFTENED

1 PLAIN MONTREAL BAGEL (PAGE 45), SPLIT AND LIGHTLY TOASTED

1 TIN SARDINES IN OLIVE OIL (ABOUT 4 SARDINES)

½ LEMON, TO FINISH

Sardines are one of the tasty little fishes that are delicious, inexpensive, and good for you. There are so many varieties to choose from, but the best come from Spain and Portugal, countries that really understand tinned fishes. Search out the best sardines packed in oil; the simplicity of the ingredients in this recipe demands that each one be spectacular. I like to top this sandwich with Quick Pickled Onions (page 166), but that's entirely optional.

Spread the butter across the warm toasted bagel. Divide the sardines (and a little of the oil they are packed in) between the two halves of the bagel and smash the fish into the melting butter. Squeeze lemon juice over the top and serve while still warm

IF A BAGEL WERE A BURRITO

Makes 2 sandwiches

8 OZ [225 G] MEXICAN-STYLE FRESH CHORIZO LINKS, CASINGS REMOVED

2 LARGE EGGS

2 HATCH CHILE JACK BAGELS (PAGE 91), SPLIT AND SCOOPED (SEE PAGE 183)

1 RIPE AVOCADO, HALVED AND PITTED

1/4 CUP [60 G] REFRIED BEANS, WARMED

2 SLICES PEPPER JACK CHEESE

1 TO 2 TSP HOT SAUCE, FOR SERVING

PICO DE GALLO, FOR SERVING

I've always loved a savory first meal like the classic American-style Tex-Mex breakfast burrito. Combine spicy chorizo, smooth beans, and runny egg with a topping of salsa and it's breakfast gold when paired with a bagel shot through with Hatch chiles.

Line a plate with a paper towel.

In a small skillet over medium-high heat, break up the chorizo with two wooden spoons. Cook the chorizo thoroughly, about 5 minutes, and transfer with a slotted spoon to the paper towel–lined plate. Set aside.

Lower the heat to medium and warm the rendered chorizo fat until shimmering. Crack in the eggs and cook until the whites are firm, the edges are crisping, but the yolks are still runny, about 3 minutes.

While the eggs are cooking, place the four bagel halves on a cutting board. Divide the avocado among all four halves, smashing and spreading it in the scooped tunnels. Next, on the bottom halves, layer the chorizo and refried beans. Lay a fried egg over each portion of refried beans, then cover each egg with a slice of cheese. Drizzle with hot sauce, as desired, and a spoonful of pico de gallo.

Place the avocado-dressed tops on the bagel sandwiches and press slightly, just enough to break the egg yolks. Cut the sandwiches in half vertically and devour.

PUTTANESCIZZA BAGEL

Makes 2 open-faced sandwiches

2 TBSP OLIVE OIL

2 ANCHOVIES, CHOPPED

1 GARLIC CLOVE, PEELED

1 TBSP TOMATO PASTE

1 TSP DRAINED CAPERS

⅛ TSP CRUSHED RED PEPPER

1 NEW YORK BAGEL (PAGE 43), SPLIT AND SCOOPED (SEE PAGE 183)

½ CUP [56 G] SHREDDED MOZZARELLA CHEESE

16 SMALL PEPPERONI SLICES, OPTIONAL

¼ TSP DRIED OREGANO

2 TBSP FINELY GRATED PARMIGIANO-REGGIANO CHEESE

When I was a teen, my after-school pizza bagel went straight from a box in the freezer to the toaster oven and bore little resemblance to either bagels or pizza. Now that I assemble them myself with pantry-friendly ingredients, pizza bagels remain a welcome snack, whether at midnight or midday. Here, I've layered a bagel with a riff on the concentrated flavors of a traditional Puttanesca sauce, with lots of umami to make a sandwich that's grown-up and unapologetic. I included pepperoni because I love the way the slices "cup" when sizzled and the way its spicy, orange-colored grease slicks the cheese. You should take a pizza bagel in any direction that satisfies your own craving or refrigerator contents: Caponata pizza bagel? Why not? Pizza bagel bianca? Naturally. Quattro formaggi? Go for it. I once made a version with fresh figs, leftover roast potatoes, and blue cheese, and I would do it again.

Set the oven rack in the uppermost position and preheat the broiler. Line a baking sheet with foil.

In a small skillet over medium-high heat, warm the olive oil. Add the anchovies and smash them with the back of a spoon, cooking them until they dissolve into the oil. Lower the heat to medium and use a Microplane to grate the garlic directly into the skillet. Cook until fragrant, less than 1 minute. Add the tomato paste and use a whisk to stir it into the fragrant oil. Whisk and cook the sauce until smooth and emulsified, 2 to 3 minutes. Add the capers and crushed red pepper and cook for another 30 seconds to form a sauce. Remove the skillet from the heat and set aside.

Place the bagel halves cut-side up on the foil-lined baking sheet. Divide the sauce between the bagels and fill the scooped-out tunnels. Cover with the mozzarella, then the pepperoni, if using. Sprinkle the oregano and Parmigiano-Reggiano evenly over the tops.

Slide the baking sheet under the broiler until the cheese is bubbling and starting to brown, no more than 2 to 3 minutes. Remove from the oven.

Let the bagels rest for a minute or two before digging in or risk that sorry burn on the roof of your mouth.

BACK IN THE DAY BRIE AND APPLE BAGEL

Makes 2 open-faced sandwiches

1 GRANOLA BAGEL (PAGE 74), SPLIT AND SCOOPED (SEE PAGE 183)

3 TBSP MANGO OR ANOTHER CHUTNEY

1 GRANNY SMITH APPLE OR BARTLETT PEAR

ONE 4 OZ [112 G] WEDGE BRIE CHEESE, RIPE AND COLD

I'm a sucker for a hunk of Brie cheese coated in chutney and baked. It's a party throwback that my grandparents Bea and Allan served at cocktail hour, and I thought it was about the fanciest thing I had ever seen.

This recipe takes that retro appetizer and gives it the bagel sandwich treatment. Here, the green apple adds crunch and a tart finish, but a crisp, bright pear is another option. Any chutney will do, but one with a little spice is especially nice. This is not the time to use the most expensive Brie. Instead, look for a wedge sized to fit on a bagel.

Set the oven rack in the uppermost position and preheat the broiler. Line a baking sheet with foil.

Place the two bagel halves cut-side up on the baking sheet. Divide the mango chutney between the two halves and spread it in the scooped tunnels.

Use a sharp knife to remove the top and bottom of the apple and a melon baller to remove the core and seeds. Slice horizontally across the apple or pear for a round slice with a hole in the middle. Depending on the size of the fruit, try to get four to six very thin slabs of fruit. Stack them on the bagel halves.

Slice the Brie in half horizontally and place one piece on each bagel half, rind-side up. Use a paring knife to carefully cut away and remove the rind (you want to do this after the cheese is on the bagel, as it becomes too gooey and difficult to transfer without the rind).

Slide the sandwiches under the broiler until the cheese is bubbly. Watch carefully—this takes no time at all. Remove from the oven and let the cheese calm down on the bagels for a minute or two before eating so you don't burn the roof of your mouth.

PAN BAGELNAT

Makes 2 sandwiches

½ CUP [100 G] DICED RIPE RED TOMATO (FROM ABOUT 2 THICK SLICES)

½ CUP [60 G] PEELED, SEEDED, AND DICED CUCUMBER (FROM ABOUT HALF A MEDIUM CUCUMBER)

½ TSP KOSHER SALT, PLUS MORE AS NEEDED

2 TSP MINCED RED ONION

2 TBSP OLIVE OIL

¼ TSP FRESHLY GROUND BLACK PEPPER, PLUS MORE AS NEEDED

2 EGG BAGELS (PAGE 61), SPLIT AND SCOOPED (SEE PAGE 183)

½ RECIPE TUNA SALAD (PAGE 158)

8 PITTED KALAMATA OLIVES, HALVED

1 HARD-BOILED EGG, SLICED

2 RADISHES, SLICED

Pan bagnat, a sandwich that hails from the south of France, is an ideal picnic take-along. Traditionally built on crusty bread, it is wrapped and weighted after assembly so the dressing and the juices from the tuna, tomato, and olives get friendly in wonderful ways. It turns out a scooped bagel is a superb alternative for the pan bagnat. Here, it's worth it to take the extra time to meticulously chop the tomato and cucumber into small pieces, about the size of peas, to keep the salad in the sandwich and avoid it slipping out the sides.

Combine the tomato and cucumber in a colander set in the sink and then sprinkle with the salt. Let sit for 10 minutes.

Scoop the tomato-cucumber mixture into a small bowl. Add the red onion, olive oil, and pepper. Stir well, then taste and correct for salt and pepper.

For each scooped bagel, fill one half with the tomato-cucumber mixture and the other with tuna salad. Layer equal amounts of the olives, egg, and radishes atop the tomato-cucumber halves, and then confidently flip the tuna salad halves on top to form two sandwiches.

Wrap the sandwiches tightly in plastic wrap. Put a plate atop each one and press down. Place a can of beans or soup or a something of a similar weight on top of each plate to compress the sandwiches. Let them rest, weighted, for no more than 1 hour at room temperature, then serve.

THANKSGIVING ANY DAY

Makes 2 sandwiches

2 TBSP MAYONNAISE

2 CINNAMON RAISIN BAGELS (PAGE 57), SPLIT, SCOOPED (SEE PAGE 183), AND LIGHTLY TOASTED

2 TBSP CRANBERRY SAUCE

¼ CUP [70 G] CHOW-CHOW OR CHOPPED SAUERKRAUT, OPTIONAL

4 OZ [112 G] THINLY SLICED ROASTED TURKEY

2 SLICES SMOKED GOUDA

ICEBERG LETTUCE LEAVES

Dorie Greenspan, the fabulous baker and cookbook author, came up with a savory strata recipe made with cinnamon raisin bread, Sriracha, and leftover Thanksgiving fare. It was so unexpected and delightful, I've never forgotten it. This sandwich is a tribute to Dorie, who really knows how to balance the savory and the sweet.

Spread the mayonnaise on one half of each bagel. Spoon cranberry sauce over the mayonnaise. Add the chow-chow, if using, to the other halves. Layer the turkey, Gouda, and lettuce on the bottom halves of each bagel.

Bring the two halves of each bagel together and press down lightly. Cut them in half vertically and serve.

COLD STEAK, BIALY, AND BLUE

Makes 2 open-faced sandwiches

2 TBSP STEAK SAUCE

2 BIALYS (PAGE 67)

8 SLICES COLD GRILLED FLANK OR HANGER STEAK (ABOUT ½ LB [225 G])

¼ CUP [28 G] CRUMBLED BLUE CHEESE

KOSHER SALT

FRESHLY GROUND BLACK PEPPER

I'm a fool for a leftover steak sandwich; it's the primary reason I grill a flank or hanger steak. Both are among the more inexpensive cuts of beef and are flavorful with a great chew—which is exactly how I describe a bialy. Blue cheese is a natural addition here, as is a little bit of steak sauce, for which I have a particular affinity. If that's not your thing, omit it, but I like the snappy zing. The amount of salt and pepper needed will be dependent on the steak's seasoning. This sandwich is terrific made with sliced roast beef from the deli too.

Spread the steak sauce across the top of each bialy and top each with 4 slices of steak. Sprinkle the blue cheese over each portion, then season with salt and pepper.

Cut each bialy in half vertically and serve.

AN ITALIAN HERO BAGEL

Makes 2 sandwiches

¼ CUP [60 G] HOT PEPPER RELISH

2 ASIAGO CHEESE AND PEPPERONI BAGELS (PAGE 87), SPLIT AND SCOOPED (SEE PAGE 183)

4 OZ [112 G] THINLY SLICED BRESAOLA

4 OZ [112 G] THINLY SLICED CAPICOLA

4 OZ [112 G] SLICED ROASTED TURKEY

4 OZ [112 G] SLICED PROVOLONE

OLIVE OIL, FOR DRIZZLING

½ CUP [30 G] PACKED ARUGULA

½ TSP DRIED ITALIAN SEASONING

It's a marriage made in heaven: a stacked Italian hero's worth of salty, chewy cured meats on a flavorful, spicy bagel. Turns out at least one particular bagel in this book is the ideal surround for salumi—made even more lively with the zing of hot pepper relish.

Spread 1 Tbsp of the hot pepper relish in each of the four bagel halves.

Divide the meats and cheese between the two bottom bagel halves, layering the bresaola, capicola, turkey, and provolone on top. Drizzle with olive oil.

In a small bowl, toss together the arugula, Italian seasoning, and another drizzle of olive oil. Divide between the two bottom halves.

Bring the two halves of each bagel together and press down lightly. Cut them in half vertically and serve.

FATTOUSH MY BAGEL

Serves 4

For the dressing

1 TBSP GROUND SUMAC, HYDRATED IN 1 TBSP WATER FOR 15 MINUTES

2 TBSP FRESHLY SQUEEZED LEMON JUICE

2 TBSP POMEGRANATE MOLASSES

1 GARLIC CLOVE

2 TSP SHERRY VINEGAR

¼ TSP KOSHER SALT

⅛ TSP FRESHLY GROUND BLACK PEPPER

¼ CUP [60 ML] OLIVE OIL

For the croutons

2 NEW YORK BAGELS (PAGE 43), SLICED VERTICALLY INTO ¼ IN [6 MM] COINS

2 TO 3 TBSP OLIVE OIL

½ TSP FLAKY SALT, SUCH AS MALDON

2 TSP ZA'ATAR

For the salad

1½ LB [680 G] LARGE, MEATY, RIPE TOMATOES (ABOUT 4)

½ TSP KOSHER SALT

1 HEAD LEAF OR BUTTER OR LITTLE GEM LETTUCE, METICULOUSLY WASHED AND DRIED

12 OZ [340 G] YOUNG, TENDER CUCUMBERS (ABOUT 3 MEDIUM)

½ CUP [58 G] SLICED RADISHES

½ CUP [30 G] CHOPPED PARSLEY

½ CUP [30 G] CHOPPED CILANTRO

¼ CUP [15 G] CHOPPED FRESH MINT

¼ CUP [15 G] THINLY SLICED SCALLIONS

½ CUP [57 G] CRUMBLED FETA CHEESE

The fattoush salad, in one form or another, can be found on mezze tables across the Middle East, Turkey, and North Africa. I make it all summer with the abundance of tomatoes, cucumbers, and fresh herbs from the garden. The classic addition of pita toasts, torn pieces of crisped pita, is replaced here with bagels, sliced into coins and lightly toasted. A variety of tomato sizes and colors makes the salad particularly inviting. Let the salad sit for a few minutes before serving to allow the bagel chips to soften and the dressing and tomato juices to mingle. The bagel croutons and the dressing may be made 1 day in advance. Refrigerate the latter and shake well before using. CONT'D

To make the dressing, combine the hydrated sumac, lemon juice, and pomegranate molasses in a small jar with a lid. Use a Microplane to grate the garlic clove right into the jar. Add the vinegar, kosher salt, and pepper, seal the jar, and shake well. Pour in the olive oil, seal, and shake again until the dressing is emulsified.

To make the croutons, line a baking sheet with parchment paper. Preheat the oven to 325°F [165°C].

In a medium bowl, use your hands to toss the bagel coins with the olive oil and flaky salt. Scatter the bagel coins across the parchment and bake for 8 minutes, until crisp and slightly golden. Remove from the oven and immediately sprinkle with the za'atar. Let cool.

To make the salad, set a colander in the sink. Core and chop the tomatoes into a 1 in [2.5 cm] dice, place in the colander, and sprinkle with the kosher salt. Toss well and allow the tomatoes to drain for about 10 minutes.

Line a wide, shallow bowl with the lettuce, torn into bite-size pieces.

Hopefully, the cucumbers are so fresh and thin-skinned that it's possible to use a table fork to scrape vertical grooves down the length of their skins. (If the cucumber has a thick, bitter skin, peel entirely before slicing.) Cut the cucumbers in half lengthwise and slice into ¼ in [6 mm] half-moons, which, thanks to the scraping, will have a decorative edge. Add the cucumbers to the salad bowl.

Scatter the radishes, parsley, cilantro, mint, and scallions over the lettuce and cucumbers. Gather the diced tomatoes in your hands, leaving any excess moisture behind, and let them fall into the salad. Sprinkle the cheese over the top, then scatter the bagel chips everywhere.

Shake the dressing again and pour it evenly over the salad. Mix the salad together (I use my impeccably clean hands to do this; it's much more efficient). Let the fattoush rest for about 10 minutes to allow the flavors to meld. Toss it once more and serve. (Make sure every serving includes a spoonful of the juicy bits in the bottom of the bowl.)

PANZABAGELLA

Serves 4

For the vinaigrette

¼ CUP [60 ML] OLIVE OIL

2 GARLIC CLOVES, CRUSHED

2 TBSP RED WINE VINEGAR

½ TSP DRIED OREGANO

For the croutons

½ CUP [120 ML] OLIVE OIL

2 GARLIC CLOVES

4 ANCHOVIES, CHOPPED

1 TBSP TOMATO PASTE

⅛ TSP CRUSHED RED PEPPER

2 NEW YORK BAGELS (PAGE 43), TORN INTO GRAPE-SIZE PIECES

For the salad

2 LB [1 KG] ASSORTED RIPE TOMATOES, CORED AND CUT INTO BITE-SIZE PIECES

½ CUP [30 G] PACKED BASIL LEAVES

¼ CUP [35 G] MINCED RED ONION

KOSHER SALT AND FRESHLY GROUND BLACK PEPPER

Panzanella pairs a tomato salad with torn bagels flavored with umami-rich oil that soak up the tomato juices. Choose a variety of tomato sizes and colors for the prettiest salad. The vinaigrette may be made ahead and refrigerated for 1 week. The croutons should be made at the last minute, so they are hot when the salad is served.

To make the vinaigrette, in a small saucepan over medium-high heat, warm the olive oil until shimmering. Turn the heat to low and drop in the garlic cloves, warming for 5 minutes. Turn off the heat and let the oil cool in the pan for 20 minutes. Discard the garlic cloves.

In a small, lidded jar, add the garlicky olive oil, red wine vinegar, and oregano and shake until combined.

To make the croutons, in a wide, nonstick skillet over medium-high heat, warm the oil until it shimmers. Cook the whole garlic cloves in the hot oil for 1 to 2 minutes, just until they begin to color. Remove the garlic and add the anchovies, tomato paste, and crushed red pepper, stirring until saucy. Lower the heat to medium and add the bagel pieces in a single layer. Let them toast, shaking the pan to flip the pieces. Continue until the croutons are barely crisped on the edges, 4 or 5 minutes at the most. Remove from the heat.

To assemble the salad, place the tomatoes in a wide, shallow serving bowl and tear the basil leaves over the top. Add the red onion, season with salt and pepper, and toss the salad well.

Add the warm croutons, then pour the vinaigrette over the top to coat. Let the salad rest for 15 minutes and serve.

PANZABAGELLA
page 195

COLD STEAK, BIALY, AND BLUE
page 191

FATTOUSH MY BAGEL
page 193

BACK IN THE DAY
BRIE AND APPLE BAGEL
page 189

PUTTANESCIZZA BAGEL
page 188

NOSHING WITH
THE FISHES
page 186

BAGEL-CENTRIC MENUS

A bagel brunch is a beautiful thing. Like so many meals organized around family traditions, there will be mandatory items on my table that may not fit in at yours. Start with bagels and a schmear and from there, add what sounds good to you. Here are a few ideas, whether it's two people or twenty at your table. Gather with loved ones and bring on the delicious.

JUST THE TWO OF US

Serves 2

2 Bagels (Your Choice)

Balaboosta Cream Cheese 103
Home-Cured Lox 143
Smoked Trout Spread. 163
Quick Pickled Onions 166
Sliced tomatoes
Capers
Lemon wedges

THE ULTIMATE DELI PLATTER AND BAGEL BRUNCH

Serves 8

Family Favorites

Cold Spinach Borscht. 176
Allan Kadetsky's Onions and Eggs . 177

Bagels

6 New York Bagels 43
with various toppings
3 Cinnamon Raisin 57
or Egg 61
or Pumpernickel 51
or Marble Bagels 55
6 Bialy 67
or 1 Pletzel 63

Fishes

Home-Cured Lox 143
Smoked Whitefish Salad 162
Smoked Sable
Smoked Sturgeon

Schmears

Balaboosta Cream Cheese 103
Chive Cheese 107
Hot-Smoked Salmon Cheese. 112
Olive Cheese 113
or Veggie Cheese. 115
Walnut Raisin Cheese. 125
Cannoli Cheese 129

Assorted Garnishes

Sliced tomatoes and cucumbers
Radishes
Thinly sliced onions (sweet or red)
Capers
Lemon wedges

YOM KIPPUR BREAK-FAST

Serves 12

Summer Beet Borscht 173

Bagels

1 dozen New York Bagels 43
with various toppings

1 dozen Montreal Bagels 45

1 Pletzel 63

Fishes

Home-Cured Lox 143

Kippered, or Hot-Smoked, Salmon . 146

Creamed Herring

Smoked Whitefish Salad 162

Schmears

Schmear Master Recipe 105

Chive Cheese 107

Horseradish Dill Cheese 112

Veggie Cheese 115

Cherry Cheesecake Cheese 127

Tamari Almond Candied Ginger Cheese 132

Ferments & Salads

Carrot Pineapple Raisin Salad 165

Quick Pickled Onions 166

Half and Full Sour Pickles 169

Panzabagella 195

AN OFFERING AT SHIVA

Serves 16

Bagels

2 each Plain, Onion, Salt, Sesame, Poppy, and Everything New York Bagels 43

6 Montreal Bagels 45

4 Bialys 67

Schmears

Balaboosta Cream Cheese 103

Chive Cheese 107

Hot-Smoked Salmon Cheese 112

Carrot Cake Cheese 126

Fish

Beet-Cured Gravlax 149

Smoked Whitefish Salad 162

Herring

Ferments & Salads

Egg Salad 154

Quick Pickled Onions 166

Half Sour Pickles 169

Spicy Marinated Olives 172

Fattoush My Bagel 193

Sliced tomatoes and cucumbers

TSURIS MIT YOYKH IZ GRINGER VI TSURIS ON YOYKH.
(TROUBLES WITH SOUP ARE EASIER THAN TROUBLES WITHOUT SOUP.) —YIDDISH SAYING

BIBLIOGRAPHY

Of all the absolute joys I encountered while writing this book, when I would begin researching with the intention to find a quick reference, that simple search would expand into entire afternoons reading about bread baking in fifteenth-century Poland or how sesame seeds grow. The rabbit holes were delicious. I also pored over recipe cards I inherited from both grandmothers and my mother, which informed my recipes, my prose, and my appreciation for all things appetizing.

Berg, Gertrude, and Waldo, Myra. *The Molly Goldberg Jewish Cookbook.* Garden City, New York: Doubleday & Company, Inc., 1955.

Engle, Fannie, and Blair, Gertrude. *The Jewish Festival Cookbook.* New York: David McKay Company, 1954.

Greenberg, Betty D., and Silverman, Althea O. *The Jewish Home Beautiful.* New York: The Women's League of the United Synagogue of America, 1941.

Gross, Aaron S., Myers, Jody, and Rosenblum, Jordan D., eds. *Feasting and Fasting: The History and Ethics of Jewish Food.* New York: New York University Press, 1997.

Kander, Mrs. Simon. *The Way to a Man's Heart: The Settlement Cookbook.* Milwaukee, Wisconsin: The Settlement Cook Book Company, 1925 and 1945 editions.

Katchor, Ben. *The Dairy Restaurant.* New York: Nextbook Press, 2020.

Maxwell, Sarah. *The Ultimate Bagel Cookbook.* Edison, New Jersey: Chartwell Books,1995.

Merwin, Ted. *Pastrami on Rye: An Overstuffed History of the Jewish Deli.* New York: New York University Press, 2015.

Nathan, Joan. *Jewish Cooking in America.* New York: Alfred A. Knopf, 1994.

Roden, Claudia. *The Book of Jewish Food: An Odyssey from Samarkand to New York.* New York: Alfred A. Knopf, 1997.

Sheraton, Mimi. *The Bialy Eaters: The Story of a Bread and a Lost World.* New York: Broadway Books, 2000.

Sinai Temple Sisterhood. *What Foods These Morsels Be.* Michigan City, Indiana: Foster Printing Services, 1954.

Women of the Ann Arbor Chapter of Hadassah. *Like Mama Used to Make: A Collection of Favorite and Traditional Jewish Dishes.* Detroit: Michigan Book Binding Company, 1952.

Zeigelman, Jane. *97 Orchard.* New York: HarperCollins, 2011.

ACKNOWLEDGMENTS

Creating a cookbook takes a creative, diligent team all the way along, from the first nugget of an idea to the last bit of grammatical tidying. At the beginning, there was my agent. Before she was my agent, Karen Murgolo was my editor. She believed in me and in this book. Karen brought me to Chronicle Books, which turned out to be the perfect pairing. When Karen left agenting to return to editing, Jon Michael Dargas took over. They've both been sounding boards and problem solvers, exactly what I needed when I needed it.

Editing, tidying, and helping me expand ideas, Cristina Garces understood the joy in this book from the first moment we talked it over (though including a pizza bagel and bagel dog took some convincing). She helped me frame the contents and guided me through endless versions of the table of contents. She encouraged me to write more about my family and to let myself be a little funny here and there. We ended every phone call talking about dogs and knitting, as it should be. Lizzie Vaughan brought the fun and designed a book that's friendly, readable, and utterly charming, then stayed at my side through the photography to make sure our vision was realized.

These recipes benefit from the inspired photography of Linda Xiao, who brought her precise and educated eye to every shot.

Barrett Washburne zhuzhed up the food, showing his skills at every step with styling magic, and Maeve Sheridan surrounded the bagels with chic props.

Thanks go to Bonnie Benwick, my good friend, solid sounding board, and first reader. Bonnie is thoughtful and sharp, and nudged me to expand, delete, and improve what was there, with an especially keen eye to the recipes.

Testers make a cookbook reliable. Across the country, better bagels were baked by Abbie and Leo Argersinger; D. Paul Brown and Sean Timberlake; Courtney Carlson, David Yarkin, Anna, Ben, and Sammy; Gail Dosik (my personal Baking 411 who went above and beyond, earning the Best Tester award); Carol Sacks, Matthew Stotts, and Claire Stotts; Jamie Samons; and Stephanie Zarpas. Thanks go to David Lebovitz who tested my bagel recipes in France, offering feedback that will help bakers here, there, and everywhere. And to Chicago-born Marilyn Naron, thank you for pointing me to the Lox Boxes and the pletzel.

Alexandra Mudry Till helped nail a bagel without gluten that still had a crisp exterior shell. The recipe was graciously tested by Carol Blymire, who knows more about GF baking than anyone I know. In the last minutes of final edits, Gayle Wald baked a batch too.

Libby Rasmussen and Lauren Frager were generous with social media advice. Frederick neighbors Kathy and Tom Hundley and Lucia, Brian, and Charlotte Hall were willing to accept porch-delivered bagels, schmears, salads, and more, day or night.

I'll always be grateful to Deb King from Deb's Artisan Bakehouse in Middletown, Maryland, who sold me 50 pounds [23 kg] of high-gluten flour at the beginning of the 2020 pandemic lockdown.

Good friends Jennifer Steinhauer and Jonathan Weisman baked bagels at home and offered excellent edits, and tasted dozens of schmears, salads, and more, providing a world of encouragement, including, but not limited to, Sunday afternoon cocktails.

My grandmothers, great-grandmothers, and my inimitable mother, Jan, were muses all of my life. I miss them all so much, quirky as they were.

And to my love, Dennis, who enthusiastically supported me through preserves, pies and pies, and now bagels: I couldn't do any of this without you. Thank you thank you thank you.

INDEX

C

D

E

F

G

Thank You — Come Again